Branding America

By Noelle Nikpour

Dedicated to Andrea Davidson Rockefeller and Katherine Rockefeller Eades, who encouraged me to write this book.

Table of Contents

- 1 -

America the Branded

Being from Arkansas, I know from experience what the expression "deer in the headlights" means. That's what happens when you come across Bambi in the middle of the highway, and she looks up from whatever she is doing and stares at you, unable to comprehend that the presence of those two yellow lights means your car is headed straight toward her.

That's what I must have looked like to the camera operator the first time I appeared as a guest commentator on Fox News on August 11, 2008.

I had found my way to this uncomfortable spot thanks to my work as a national Republican political fundraiser. I had done extensive work for various campaigns, most recently as an 18-state coordinator for Rudy Giuliani's presidential race – a race I still can't believe we lost, but more on that later. Not long after the campaign ended, I was running on a treadmill at my gym and watching Fox News when I saw a friend and former coworker being interviewed on TV. I couldn't believe someone I knew was on my screen, so I texted her my congratulations. Soon afterwards, she texted me back. "Oh, my gosh, where are you?" she wrote. "You would be so great at this. You need to come to New York and talk to some people in the television business."

With my candidate out of the race and time on my hands, I soon followed her advice, headed to New York, and talked to some producers. All I had going for me was that I knew what I was talking about when it came to Republican Party politics, fundraising and strategy. They agreed to put me on twice: a brief interview on an afternoon news show, and then most of a full hour on "Red Eye," a live talk show that aired at 3 a.m. and featured celebrities and political types spouting opinions and making jokes about current events.

It all sounded fun. I thought I could do it. And then, that afternoon, the camera light came on.

The host – who it was I can't remember – asked me a question, which I also can't remember. It probably was about Barack Obama. I do remember opening my mouth and spitting out some nonsensical answer as my brain shifted back and forth from whatever I was talking about to the fact that millions of people were watching me. Directors in the background were making slashing motions in front of their throats. As soon as I took a breath, the host cut to a commercial, and I was escorted off the set. They told me I was terrible and began trying to figure out how to get me off of that night's "Red Eye" before I put even the nation's worst insomniacs to sleep.

For some reason, they decided to give me one more chance, and what had been a one-day lark suddenly became a fight for survival. Before, I had been a political fundraiser appearing on TV for fun. Now I wanted to prove that I could perform, just as I had proven myself as a Republican fundraiser despite living in Arkansas, which until recently was one of the most Democratic states in the union.

So there I was at 3 a.m. sitting next to Fox News Channel anchor Patti Anne Brown and "Red Eye" regular Bill Schulz while comedian Greg Proops was in some studio on the Left Coast. All of them had extensive television experience. Proops had been a semi-regular on Drew Carey's ABC improvisational comedy, "Who's Line Is It, Anyway?" Host Greg Gutfeld showed a clip of two silly kids lip-synching to some song and then introduced us, pointing out that I was a first-time guest.

Gutfield started the show by interviewing the National Enquirer reporter who broke the story of Democratic presidential candidate John Edwards' affair with a campaign aide. Then he turned to me and said, "Noelle, do you think the media was right not to cover this story until Edwards confirmed the affair?"

I had learned my lesson. In television, you don't have time to think about your answer. You have a split second to come up with something direct and to the point, and after the previous afternoon's debacle, I knew I couldn't blow it again. "No! I think that the media should have gone on and gone with it, but they were protecting their beloved, uhh, shining star Democrat," I said. "You know, they do not want to say anything about a Democrat, for God's sake."

OK, so it won't go down as one of broadcast television's great moments, but I had managed to sound coherent enough that I wasn't thrown off the set. The hour flew by. It was goofy and fun. The show covered everything from politics to vampire bats to the most painful way to be executed. It was like a conversation among friends around the table late at night when we all probably ought to be in bed. I learned to forgive myself when I said something that came out wrong and move on quickly.

I was the only political professional and the most opinionated person on the set. Of course Arkansas got brought up – how could it not with my accent? I laughed it off. After all, I had a role to play: I was a kinder, gentler, Southern Ann Coulter.

And that's where Noelle Nikpour's brand was born.

Within a couple of weeks of that appearance, I started getting calls to appear on other programs. I soon appeared many times on "Red Eye" as well as other shows, including Fox's "Hannity," HLN's "Showbiz Tonight," and CNBC's "Power Lunch" – shows, by the way that also are brands. The South Florida Sun-Sentinel invited me to be a political columnist for their newspaper.

I realized that while there may be people who know more about certain issues than I do, they weren't as good at delivering a punch in an entertaining way. When you're on television, you don't have time to call upon your vast store of knowledge and then boil it down so the viewers can understand. You've got to get in and get out – one idea, one fact, hopefully delivered memorably, and often said in 45 seconds with some director talking in your ear. You either have it or you don't, and if you don't, they don't tell you how to get it. There is no political punditry school, and it's a tough world. It's reality TV based on politics. It's professional wrestling without the folding chairs, except there's nothing scripted about what we do. Another major difference: It's the job of professional wrestlers to make each other look good. Not so with us. Most of us political pundits are friendly to each other in the back room. We ask each other what we did that weekend. We smile and drink coffee and talk. And then we go out there in front of the camera and try to rip each other apart. Afterwards it's usually OK. If one got the best of the other, we come off the set, discuss it a little more, and move on. After all, I'm a very nice person except for the five minutes when I'm arguing my side's case.

As my fundraising career became a fundraising/media career, I realized how important my personal brand was to my success. The fact that I could argue a conservative Republican point of view, but do it with a smile, gave television producers a reason to put me on the air. My Southern accent softened everything I said. I could verbally punch Obama in the nose and sound like I was offering him a slice of sweet potato pie. The fact that I was on television reminded campaigns that I might be worth hiring. Some donors, too, were more willing to open their wallets when the person asking for their money had been on TV.

Branding is a fact of modern life. It's how products get sold in a very crowded marketplace, and it's how minor celebrities become major ones.

Take, for example, Paris Hilton. Before 2003, everyone had heard of the hotel heiress's last name but no one had heard of her. She did not even complete high school, though she did later earn her G.E.D. She was the personification of unearned wealth. She dabbled in modeling but mostly in partying. She made a sex tape with her boyfriend that she apparently never meant to see the light of day. Aside from her looks, name and money, she apparently didn't have much to offer the world.

Except this: She was a brand waiting to happen.

Beneath the party girl exterior was an ambitious businesswoman who told the New York Times in April 2005 at the age of 24 that she was "glad I got the partying out of my system when I was young, because now I'm so over it and I can focus on my career. Now I'm trying to build an empire. I don't want to be known as this Hilton hotel girl my whole life. I want to make my own name."[1]

For Hilton, the name would be the empire. She took her two redeeming qualities – her looks and her last name – and then used them to create a ditzy celebrity brand that would offend Americans so much that they couldn't help but pay attention to her. Step by step – and this was no accident – she made herself into America's number one empty, spoiled rich girl. She teamed up with childhood friend Nicole Ritchie, the daughter of singer Lionel Ritchie, for a television show called "The Simple Life" in which the two left their Beverly Hills lifestyle behind and lived on a farm in Arkansas, basically messing up everything because they had no idea how to work or follow the rules.

The show continued in one form or another for five years, and while the ratings were OK, they were nothing compared to what was happening in Hilton's real life at the same time. That "show" was far more interesting. It featured her landing over and over again in the headlines – for the sex tape, for the well-publicized ending of her friendship with Ritchie, for her well-publicized romantic relationships, and for her well-publicized minor run-ins with the law. The press ate it up. Barbara Walters named her one of "The 10 Most Fascinating People of 2004." The 2007 Guinness Book of World Records called her the "World's Most Overrated Celebrity." During the 2008 presidential campaign, Sen. John McCain made a highly successful ad correlating Obama to Hilton and another famous ditz, singer Brittney Spears. Hilton responded with an ad of her own in which she announced she was running for president. As she told the Times, "If you want to make fun of yourself and play into the whole stereotype, then why not? I have a hit show. Obviously I know what I'm doing."[2]

In addition to the money she was raking in for "The Simple Life," she began introducing her own lines of clothing, jewelry, perfume and fitness facilities. Her books became best-sellers. At one point, she made $150,000 to $200,000 appearing for 20 minutes at a party. She recorded albums and appeared in movies. Marketing consultant Al Ries, chairman of Ries and Ries, told the Times that she was "the Donald Trump of the younger generation." "She's definitely got good instincts, and she understands the power of being in the public eye," he said. "You don't have to have stories saying nice things about you; you just have to have stories saying something about you."[3]

The Paris Hilton model has since been followed by other wealthy socialites, most notably Hilton's friend, Kim Kardashian, who made her own sex tape and stars in her own reality show, "Keeping Up With the Kardashians," which gives viewers a peak into her charmed and over-dramatic life. Like Hilton, Kardashian is everywhere, always in the news, and always making money. Even her wedding, which resulted in a 72-day marriage, was a financial transaction thanks to payments from the television show and wedding photos by People magazine.[4] She has her own clothing, jewelry and perfume lines.

Hilton and Kardashian are the results of a process that started in the 1800s and progressed through the television age and today's Web 2.0. While the tools for branding are changing, what's revolutionary is the fact that everything now is being branded, including celebrities and, increasingly, politicians and political parties. Candidates going back to the Founding Fathers had a brand, but branding reached a new level – some might say a new low – in 2008 with the empty but brilliant candidacy of Barack Obama, a man thoroughly unqualified to be president but wonderfully qualified for a modern presidential campaign.

Now branding has moved beyond the rich and famous into our everyday lives. More and more, individuals are learning what Paris Hilton figured out long ago. People have always made money by calling attention to themselves, even if it not for very good reasons. But in today's world, when everyone has a website and a blog, when everyone posts on Facebook and Twitter, it's even more important. As Americans spend more and more time online, they are increasingly using some of the same branding techniques used by celebrities and politicians. If attention is the economy of the web and if so many of us are living there, then it's not just companies, millionaire hotel heiresses and politicians who must brand themselves, but the rest of us as well. The painter Andy Warhol once said, "In the future, everyone will be famous for 15 minutes." This is the future he was talking about, but instead of being famous, everyone is simply branded.

What's your brand? Whether you want one or not, you have one. Each of us comes into contact with thousands of people a week, so there's no way we can understand each of them in all their complexity. So we take shortcuts. Think about the people you know – your friends in real life and on Facebook. Somebody is the funny guy. The nice older gentlemen. The bitch. The churchgoing mom. They're all more than that, of course, but you can't possibly process that much information, at least not when you are scrolling up and down your Facebook page or sorting through the relationships in your life.

Guess what? Everyone – your friends, your acquaintances, your employer/clients and your potential employer/clients – is doing the same to you. They don't have time to process all of the subtle nuances that make you such a wonderful person. You will be defined. So define yourself first.

Clare Boothe Luce, the journalist, playwright and ambassador, said, "A great man is one sentence."[5] As Reagan speechwriter Peggy Noonan later explained, that means that presidents must concentrate on certain areas if they want to have a lasting impact. Her boss reduced government and helped win the Cold War. George Washington is the father of our country. Abraham Lincoln ended slavery and preserved the union.[6]

What's your sentence? Consciously and subconsciously, you project an image in the actual and online worlds that directly affects the jobs you get, the lifestyle you lead, the influence you have, and the friends you make and keep. It's your responsibility to make sure your image accurately reflects the person you are – or better yet, authentically reflects the person you aspire to be.

- 2 -

Marketing vs. Branding

Almost everyone remembers the Pepsi Challenge.

The series of TV commercials during the 1970s and 1980s featured blind taste tests where cola drinkers snatched from the street chose Pepsi over Coke. They always looked surprised, as if their tongues had been so scalded by years of drinking acidic carbonated water that they wouldn't know their favorite soda from another until they saw the labels.

The campaign was successful. Pepsi cut into Coke's lead in the cola wars. Spooked Coke executives decided to change the formula and, in 1985, rolled out a sweeter version of the drink that most people came to call "new Coke." Lovers of the old Coca-Cola rebelled. Within a couple of months, the company brought back the old formula as Coca-Cola Classic. Now consumers can't even buy the product known as Coke II in the United States.

The Pepsi Challenge was one of the most successful advertising campaigns in memory. By contrast, in 2010, Advertising Age called new Coke "one of marketing's biggest blunders."[1]

But today Coca-Cola is by far the leading cola. In fact, in 2011 Diet Coke passed Pepsi for the number two slot.

How could a product that a majority of people once said is better than its rival now be losing to it and to its diet version? Especially considering that, for a time at least, its marketing was so much better?

There are two possible explanations. One is that Pepsi's sweeter taste wins out in a sipping contest but not when comparing the much larger quantities people actually drink. We actually like Coke better than Pepsi when we drink by the can.

But there's also this. In 2003, Dr. Reed Montague, a neuroscientist at the Baylor College of Medicine in Houston, did his own taste test. Using an MRI to monitor their brain activity, he asked 67 blindfolded subjects which they liked better, and more than half said Pepsi. Montague knew they were telling the truth because the ventral putamen, which is stimulated when a person likes how something tastes, was showing increased activity. When he told the subjects what they were sampling before they tasted it, 75 percent said they preferred Coke. This time, not only were their ventral putamens lighting up but also their medial prefrontal cortex, the home of higher thinking and discernment. Montague theorized that people saw the Coke label and gravitated to the brand they trusted.[2]

That's the power of branding, and nobody has a better brand than Coke. It's "The Real Thing," after all. In fact, Interbrand, the world's largest brand consultancy firm, said in 2011 that Coca-Cola is the most valuable brand in the world, just as it has been every year since 2001. Pepsi is number 22 on the list.[3]

Branding is the creation of a relationship between a product – a consumer good, a political campaign, a celebrity, an individual – and the consumer. The word "brand" derives from the Old Norse word "brandr," which meant "to burn" and referred to the practice of Vikings branding their animals to identify them. Later cultures also used branding to mark their property, and of course, everyone associates branding with cattle ranchers who have used it for centuries to identify their stock.[4] Like cowboys in the Old West, marketers try to stamp their product into our brains by making what marketers call a brand promise that it will fulfill a particular need. Doing this is not cheap. An estimated $654 billion, nearly $300 billion of that in the United States, was spent on branding in 2008.[5]

Branding is more than marketing. Marketing touts a product; branding creates a relationship. According to Scott Margenau with the branding firm Imageworks Studio, "If marketing is doing, then branding is being."[6] In other words, marketing is communicating, while branding is positioning. Marketing shouldn't be minimized – it's almost impossible to brand without marketing. But it's not enough. Effective branding tells a story starring the consumer and the product as the main characters. It involves not only the advertising but the packaging, the logos, the name, the fonts, the sales staff, the vibe the company gives off, and the product itself. You don't fly Southwest just because a television commercial told you it has the lowest fares. You also fly it because it actually does have the lowest fares, and because everything about the experience – from the fact that the bags fly free to the way the airline loads its passengers to the funny way that the flight attendants give their preflight instructions – reinforces Southwest's brand. Southwest is a safe, dependable, laid back, no frills airline for people who are too smart to get caught up in all the drama associated with the other carriers, and that's why people choose it.

To see the real difference between good marketing and good branding, look no farther than the Segway scooter, if you can find one.[7] The marketing for the Segway during its development was brilliant. For years, Americans heard vaguely that a revolutionary product, known only as "It," was being created that would change everything. Everyone was wondering what "It" was. Then the Segway was released to a barrage of publicity. Since humans were created, walking has been our principle means of transportation, and this supposedly was going to change it. We were told we all would be riding one of these things.

Good marketing, bad branding. The Segway is an amazing product that has failed to live up to its brand promise. We were told that it would change our lives. Instead, unless you work in a certain profession – maybe as a security guard or a package deliverer in a city with good sidewalks – you don't really need it. We were told that it was a safe product. Then the company's CEO died in 2010 after riding one of the machines off a cliff. Over time, more professions may figure out how to utilize it. It eventually may be modified to become a very effective tool for helping senior citizens and people with disabilities live more mobile lives. But that's not how it was branded.

In his book, BrandSimple, Allen Adamson, managing director of the New York brand consultancy and design firm Landor Associates, described what makes a brand successful: It must be different and relevant, with difference being the more important of the two. Relevance just means the product or service is available and needed, like Kmart, which sells the same crap made in China that everyone else sells. Walmart, on the other hand, is cheaper and has everything a shopper needs under one roof, which makes it different.[8]

For a branding effort to be successful, it must have an effective brand driver – a single phrase or sentence that quickly captures a product's essence and is so simple that it almost cannot be miscommunicated – like Walmart's "Everyday low prices," reinforced for so many years by the company's founder, Sam Walton, an everyday low prices kind of guy. "The most powerful brands in the world, whether they're big brands or small, are based on clear, gut-simple ideas," Adamson wrote.[9]

Here's one clear, gut-simple idea: Be the most affordable hotel. Many travelers want only a bed, a TV, and a clean bathroom, and for them, Motel 6 won that space years ago. Born in 1962, the chain has frugality encoded in its DNA. In fact, the "6" comes from the $6 per night rates the motel originally charged its customers. Starting in 1986, the company began employing Tom Bodett as its national spokesperson.[10] Already a radio personality, he was hired because he sounded like the kind of person who would stay at a Motel 6 – which he, in fact, says he does. Bodett's down-to-earth style reinforces the idea that Motel 6 is the no-nonsense choice for budget-minded travelers. The famous tag line, "We'll leave the light on for you," which Bodett ad-libbed while recording a spot, takes the edge off. Instead of Motel 6 being just a cheap hotel, it's your neighborhood innkeeper.

Bodett told Advertising Age in 2007 that travelers feel vulnerable and don't want to be tricked into paying for things they don't need. Staying at a Motel 6 makes them feel like they have outsmarted the whole racket. "Americans are generally very self-sufficient and, I think, generally averse to pretension, just as I am," he said. "When you point out that you don't need to have art on your motel room walls because your eyes are closed anyway, or that you can take the money you save from not having avocado body balm in the bathroom swag basket and go buy some real chips and dip – avocado body balm, by the way, tastes just like soap – people respond."[11]

So where did all of this branding come from?

Branding didn't really exist during the country's earliest years, when Americans produced most of what they needed with their own hands. Modern marketing began to take shape, mostly through simple packaging, rudimentary advertising, and slogans, in the 18th and 19th centuries as Americans purchased more and more brand-name goods in stores.[12]

In the 20th century, the tools of mass communication – television, radio, and print media – enabled advertisers to reach the masses, and generally the masses were open to being reached. Those media, particularly television, had come of age during a time of relative national consensus following World War II. The public had not been inundated with advertising since childhood and therefore had no reason to be distrustful. Moreover, marketers could be assured that, with only NBC and CBS to choose from, a significant percentage of consumers would be tuned into the show on which they advertised. Since those consumers didn't have remote controls, they likely would watch the commercial.

By the 1960s, Americans were growing less trusting of advertising. Young people watching their friends go overseas to fight in a questionable war were being told not to trust anyone over 30, which included a lot of ad executives. Marketers learned to break through the walls consumers had built up by using humor, manipulative techniques, and, of course, shock-and-awe firepower. Today the average 66-year-old American will have viewed two million television commercials in his or her lifetime – the equivalent of six years of 56-hour workweeks.[13] The market research firm Yankelovich guessed in the mid-2000s that a typical city dweller was exposed to up to 5,000 ads per day, compared to 2,000 just 30 years earlier.[14] Amidst this onslaught, the average consumer will remember only 1-3 percent of these ads without prompting.[15] What they do remember, they aren't likely to trust. In 2009, Yankelovich reported that 76 percent of Americans believed that advertisers didn't tell the truth.[16]

Not surprisingly, Americans were becoming annoyed with all of this advertising and embraced technology that helped them to avoid it. Digital video recorders enabled them to record their favorite shows, news and live sporting events, happily skipping the commercials that were paying for their free entertainment. That meant that advertisers no longer had 30 seconds to convince viewers to buy their product. They might have three seconds to give them a reason to watch the commercial. Recently, Dish Network, which has more than 14 million subscribers, struck what could be a fatal blow to the advertising model by introducing Auto Hop, which enables viewers to skip commercials entirely. Instead of having to fast-forward through ads – which, by the way, are being designed to communicate a message even when fast-forwarded

– viewers with Auto Hop simply see a black screen throughout the commercial break.[17] Broadcasters are suing.

Meanwhile, viewership is becoming more and more dissipated. Not too long ago there were three networks, and everyone in America knew who "The Fonz" was. Now there are hundreds of channels clamoring for the attention of viewers, who might be surfing the internet at the same time they are watching the show. American Idol, the top-rated prime time show during the week of January 23, 2012, attracted only 11 percent of the nation's TV homes.[18]

In this environment, it no longer is cost-effective for advertisers simply to bombard us with 30-second ads and wait for us to buy. With branding, they use the entire marketing and sales process to try to stick the product permanently on our mind's shelf, hoping we'll place it on a real conveyor belt when the time comes.

Perhaps the most powerful of these branding tools is the one that has existed the longest: word of mouth. It's how all of the world's great religions were spread, including Christianity, which started with a carpenter's son with 12 followers.

Some word of mouth advertising is quite deliberate, even deceptive. Sellers hire attractive young people to hang out in front of stores to entice other young people to go inside. I'm sure you are familiar with the Central Intelligence Agency. Ever heard of the Girls Intelligence Agency? That's the company that recruits 40,000 girls across the United States to talk up their products among their friends and classmates.[19]

But not all word of mouth marketing involves such tactics. Much of it simply takes advantage of the fact that human beings are social creatures. In an April 2009 Nielsen Global Online Consumer Survey of more than 25,000 internet users worldwide, 90 percent said they either "completely" or "somewhat" trusted recommendations for purchasing decisions made by people they knew. A distant second was consumer opinions posted online – by complete strangers, in other words – along with brand websites, both of which were trusted by 70 percent of respondents.[20]

That means the most important advertising occurs person to person, and while marketers can't control that process, they can guide it by producing content that encourages conversations about their product – not just any conversations, mind you, but conversations that lead people to talk about their brands within their spheres of influence. In other words, the right people talking to each other at the right time. In their 2012 book, "The Face-to-Face Book," professional word-of-mouth marketers Ed Keller and Brad Fay point to companies such as TOMS Shoes, which has spent very little on advertising but has generated tremendous word of mouth by donating a pair of shoes to a person in need for each pair bought retail. Another successful word-of-mouth advertiser is Chick-fil-A, whose Christian management requires locations to be closed on Sundays and has instituted a "Daddy-Daughter Date Night" where restaurants are closed to the general public and the red carpet is literally rolled out for fathers and daughters spending a special evening together. Nintendo introduced its Wii gaming platform to age groups beyond the typical teenage boy cohort in part by recruiting influential women to host parties for their friends. Later the game consoles were placed on cruise ships, in senior citizen facilities and elsewhere.[21]

Successful word of mouth marketing involves not only masses of people but also the right people. In 2003, Keller and fellow marketing researcher Jon Berry published "The Influentials," which made this provocative statement on its cover: "One American in ten tells the other nine how to vote, where to eat, and what to buy." The book made the case that 10 percent of Americans who were socially, professionally and politically engaged set the tone for the rest of the nation.[22] A few years earlier, the writer Malcolm Gladwell described in his book, "The Tipping Point," how Hush Puppies shoes, which had been in decline, suddenly became popular in the mid-1990s – not because of some major marketing campaign, but because a few influential kids in New York started wearing them, and it spread from there.[23] In Martin Lindstrom's book "Brandwashed," the author described an experiment conducted by Leeds University researchers in which subjects were told to wander around a large hall without talking, with a few given instructions on where they should walk. Soon the others were following those who looked like they knew what they were doing. The researchers concluded that five percent of what they called "informed individuals" could influence up to 200 people.[24]

Other branding techniques incorporate the use of what are known as "unconscious signals" to create cravings for a product. Companies spend big bucks to engineer a particular sound when the bottle opens or when the car door shuts. How important are these signals? Imagine yourself drinking a Coca-Cola. Want one? Maybe a little. Now imagine holding a bright red can in your hand and seeing the beads of water along its side. Now you open the top and hear the "phhff!" sound as the carbon is released. Pour the contents into a glass of ice and listen to that unmistakable sound as it fills. See the foam rise almost to the top. Stick a straw inside. Now do you want a Coca-Cola? Those are unconscious signals. At one time, Pepsi was studying how it could engineer its cans to emit a sweet smell or spray a water mist when drinkers popped open a can.[25]

Those branding signals engage senses other than the eyes. Sounds can have a powerful effect on consumers' purchasing decisions. For one study at the University of Leicester, researchers alternately played French and German music in the wine section of a supermarket. You guessed it – customers bought more French wines on French music days and more German wines on German music days.[26] Sonic beams that cover only a few feet radius and seem as though they are coming from inside a person's head can be used near product displays, bringing to mind the "Saturday Night Live" "Mr. Subliminal" character from a few years back who was able to get whatever he wanted by subtly fitting that request into the middle of a casual conversation.[27] The way an iPod feels in your hand can make you more inclined to buy it. Odor is a powerful force because it is the sense with the most connections between its region of the brain and the amygdala-hippocampal complex, seat of emotional memories.[28] In short, we're dogs with less hair. Well, most of us, anyway. Marketers know this and can use it to their advantage as long as the effect is congruous and pleasant – baby powder in a place selling nursery items, for example, but not in the auto care department. Fast food restaurants pipe a fake hamburger smell through the air vents to get us into the mood to clog our arteries.

Where could this lead in politics? Candidates have long used jingles to implant their names in voters' minds, and commercials in recent years have often featured candidates backed by stirring, even heroic music. Now it can be taken further. Could a smart candidate pipe the smell of gun oil into an NRA convention before he or she speaks? Could a female candidate implant a brochure with scents associated with motherhood and apple pie? What if, instead of holding signs at an opponent's rally, campaigns secretly pumped in a subtle but unpleasant smell? If it's possible to manipulate people, you can bet that candidates will try to figure out how.

- 3 -

The Power of Emotion: Apple vs. Microsoft

Emotion activates the brain 3,000 times faster than other thoughts, and studies have shown that shoppers will pay twice as much when basing their decisions on emotion rather than reason.[1] Branding taps into those emotions. In fact, brain scans have shown that photos of strong brands produce the same neural activity as religious images. Even sports images didn't produce as strong an image.[2] A good brand can so effectively worm its way into people's heads that they can hardly separate themselves from it. That's why in one July 2007 survey, 57 percent of Toyota Prius owners said the main reason they bought the car was, "It makes a statement about me."[3]

A good example of such effective emotional branding is Dove soap. Its branding effort starts with the product, which contains "one-quarter cleansing cream," and is reinforced with packaging and advertising that communicates the idea that using Dove soap is like taking a soft, milky, rejuvenating bath.[4]

But a bath is what you experience; beauty is what you are, and through its brilliant "Campaign for Real Beauty" branding campaign, Dove has inserted itself not only into shopping carts but into women's psyches. Dove and its partners studied more than 3,000 girls in 10 countries and found only 2 percent described themselves as beautiful. Thus began its Campaign for Real Beauty, which features normal-looking models with normal-looking bodies. The message was the exact opposite of that sent by competing advertisers featuring drop-dead gorgeous women. Those advertisers were saying, "Use our product, and you will look like this," which women knew couldn't be true, so those ads only made them feel inferior. Dove's branding campaign said, "Use our product because you, and people like you, are already beautiful." The result? During the first two years of the campaign, global sales of Dove products increased more than 10 percent.[5]

No doubt Dove's makers and marketers feel good about what they are doing, and rightfully so. But make no mistake: This is a business. Dove's parent company, Unilever, also sells the Axe family of products, which have been marketed by one of the most sexist and sexually suggestive ad campaigns in recent memory. One ad featured an average-looking young man on an island being attacked by hordes of bikini-wearing babes racing toward him like sex-starved animals from every direction. A different need is being tapped there, and no less effectively!

One of the most powerful – and most often used – emotional marketing tools is nostalgia, which is rooted in our natural desire to remember the past more positively than it actually occurred. That desire grows stronger as we grow older and can become more acute during difficult economic times, such as what the country has been experiencing the past few years. We certainly saw that when Americans flocked to familiar comfort food after the attacks of September 11, 2011.

Nostalgia works best when customers are hooked on a product when they are young, so that's what marketers try to do. Child psychologist Dr. Allen Kanner at Berkeley's Wright Institute was quoted in the book "Brandwashed" by Martin Lindstrom saying that the average American child recognizes 100 brand logos by the time he or she is three years old. A study by the Journal of Consumer Research found that children begin to understand the meaning of products and brands at about age 11 or 12, the same time of life when their self-esteem dips. Brands provide them a way to reinforce that self-esteem. For "Brandwashed," Lindstrom along with the SIS International Research firm surveyed more than 2,000 children and adults and found that half said they used brands they remembered from childhood. "In my career, I've found time and again that there is often a specific moment or time in our lives when we form such powerful memories involving a brand that we decide (subconsciously) to consume the product for life," he wrote.[6]

That makes sense. Look in your kitchen pantry and see what brands were also in your parents' pantry. I'll bet you munch on the same brand of peanut butter that your mom smeared on your PB&J. Is your kitchen cabinet stocked with Kraft Macaroni and Cheese? You know, there are cheaper alternatives with the same dried noodles and powdery processed "cheese" ingredient.

Nowhere is the power of nostalgia used more often than in politics. President Reagan was successful for a lot of reasons, not the least of which was that he was correct on the issues, but he also was a genius when it came to painting pictures of an idealized past. Now Republicans are nostalgic for Reagan. Democrats yearn for a return to John F. Kennedy's "Camelot," as mythical a place in American history as King Arthur's Camelot may have been in world history. In reality, the JFK White House was a place of intrigue and adultery. The "youthful" president was actually in poor health and not exactly faithful to his glamorous queen. "Give 'em hell" Harry Truman occasionally comes up as a reference point for both parties as well.

Fear is one of the most powerful tools available to marketers. That emotion is based in the amygdala, a small part of the brain that has a huge impact on our actions. Because it connects to so many parts of the brain while the logic area, the cortex, has so few connections, the amygdala can override virtually every part of our thought processes when it takes over. There is a very good reason for this: We don't always have time to think about the logical reasons of why we should run from the bear. But this aspect of human nature also makes us vulnerable to marketers who use our fears to get us to buy their product, service or a political candidate. Marketers employ a three-step process: identify a problem (even if they have to create it), make us worry about it, and then promise to fix it.[7] Some, of course, prey on outright fears, such as the cheesy but very effective LifeCall commercial where a helpless elderly lady used the pager system to say, "I've fallen, and I can't get up!" Creating a fear of failure is another common tactic, with the most powerful version of this fear being a future "feared self" – one that is bald, impotent, broke, overweight, and/or alone. Sometimes marketers play on the fear that we have lost control, and they can provide the comfort we lack. Add a dose of guilt and regret, and marketers can effectively spur us to action.[8]

Meanwhile, there's another reason why fear is such a powerful marketing tool: We kind of like it in the right circumstance. Fear creates adrenaline, which leads to the release of epinephrine, a hormone that can create a satisfying sensation. The areas of the brain associated with fear and pleasure are closely associated. That means when people are afraid but also know they are not in real danger, they get the benefits of all those hormones without the actual possibility of death or injury. It's the reason we like roller coasters and horror movies, and why some people like kinky sex. It's also the reason we spread scary rumors.[9]

Remember in the last chapter how we talked about how humans are social creatures? Consumers – of products, services and politics – naturally follow the crowd. In one experiment described by Lindstrom and published in the journal Science, researchers wired teenagers to an MRI and had them rate 15-second song clips. Then they told them which songs were most popular. When the teenagers' ratings reflected the overall songs' popularity, the caudate nucleus, a part of the brain associated with rewards, tended to light up. When the individual teens' selections did not match the group's, there was increased brain activity in parts of the brain associated with anxiety. Lindstrom found similar results when he hooked up women who liked Louis Vuitton handbags to an MRI. The women said they liked the bags because of their work-manship, but when shown pictures of the company's products, brain activity was prominent in the Brodmann area, associated with "cool-ness." Regardless of what they said or even what they believed, they liked them because they knew others liked them.

One of consumers' most powerful emotional needs is a desire to be a part of a community. It's no secret that many Americans feel isolated. In 2000, Robert Putnam's book, "Bowling Alone," detailed how Ameri-cans knew their neighbors less well than in the past and belonged to fewer community organizations such as bowling leagues.[10] Since Put-nam's book was published, Facebook and Twitter have enabled Ameri-cans to replace one form of community for another, but a Facebook "friend" is no substitute for one next door. The General Social Survey found that, in 2006, half of Americans said they have two or fewer friends, compared to three in 1985.[11]

Marketers know that Americans have a deep, emotional yearning to be part of a tribe, so they try to fill that void with their products. Bud-weiser drinkers comprise one part of a population and Samuel Adams drinkers another. There are plenty of men where I live down South who only drive a Ford or Chevy truck, and it's not because, year after year, they make a sophisticated value comparison. Few companies have more thoroughly made their brand a part of a lifestyle than Harley Davidson. That company might manufacture motorcycles, but what it sells is community. Harley owners are practically a country within a country and definitely their own tribe, with their own uniforms (sold by Harley) and even an unofficial creed, a kind of tough-guy patriotism not available to owners of Japanese brands such as Honda. For a Harley Davidson owner to purchase another brand would mean much more than a purchasing decision. It would mean defecting to another country.

But no company has more effectively used the power of emotion to brand its products than Apple. Apple makes a brand promise that is similar to the one that Segway made – to provide an easy-to-use, personal technology product that will change your life. But Apple is now one of the world's richest companies – and probably its most transformative – because it keeps that promise.

This did not happen overnight. Back in 1984, Steve Jobs introduced the Macintosh, promising it would be "insanely great." The famous "1984" commercial that ran during the Super Bowl implied this little computer would save the world from an IBM-inflicted Orwellian nightmare. And truly the Macintosh was an insanely great, world-changing product. It was easy to use. It was powerful. And Jobs was a great salesman. It was a heck of a brand.

The next couple of decades, however, would show the limits of branding. Bill Gates and his team at Microsoft had a better, more flexible business model, and Gates himself was a better businessman than Jobs. Microsoft's Windows operating system, while inferior to Apple's closed system, could run on any computer other than a Mac and became the industry standard. Apple's share of the market fell almost to nothing. Jobs was forced out of the company he founded. When he returned to Apple in 1997, it was on its last legs.

But while the company's business model was broken, its brand was still strong. Despite years of poor management, bad strategies and ill-conceived products, Apple was still the company that made better computers that hardly anybody used. Relevant? Barely. But different? Yeah, and as Allen Adamson told us in "BrandSimple," different is more important. In fact, one of the company's first moves that happened under

Jobs was the "Think Different" advertising campaign featuring "rebels," "troublemakers," and "ones who see things differently" such as Ghandi, Dr. Martin Luther King, and Albert Einstein. The television ads didn't feature a computer or even mention Apple's name. The only reference to the company was a brief tagline featuring the Apple logo and its slogan, "Think Different." The point was, Apple wasn't a computer company. It was a company that helped people "think different." Then Apple introduced the iMac, which became relevant because it was different. In a market in which every computer was beige or black, the iMac was a self-contained computer/monitor that came in five colors, and those colors served as a branding signal to consumers that it was fun and easy to use. One of the early commercials marketing the computer didn't even plug it in; it just showed five spinning iMacs followed by that same tagline, "Think different."

That was a powerful concept that resonated with a lot of people. Apple developed a core of users, if you'll forgive the pun, who stuck with the company for a lot of reasons, not the least of which was, like the Prius, it made a statement about them. They kept the company in business by buying Apples despite the hassles of trying to transfer files to the Windows computers everyone else had, despite the fact that Macs were more expensive, and despite the fact that most of the cool stuff couldn't run on their machines.

Year after year, Jobs stood before developers and the public and reinforced the brand by introducing innovative products. These announcements took on the tone of church revival. By the time Jobs had finished describing the "one more thing" that always came at the end of the address, the audience was practically chanting his name.

The company climbed out of near bankruptcy. Its market share inched upward, though it never had a prayer of threatening Microsoft when it came to operating systems. Gates still was the richest man in the world. Microsoft still seemed so ready to take over our lives that governments in the United States and Europe intervened to limit its power.

But while Microsoft had a better business model than Apple, it did not have a better brand. While Apple stood for people-centered computing, Microsoft simply stood for omnipresence when it came to operating systems and Office software. It was everywhere, so you had to have it, but there was no Microsoft community, no tribe except perhaps computer techies who loved it because it made the rest of us feel stupid and themselves feel smart. People who bought Windows did so because they thought they had no choice. Those who bought Macs did so for much different and more personal reasons. Microsoft was selling specific computer products – Windows, Office, etc. Apple was selling the ability to think differently.

Then in 2001, Jobs stood before the MacWorld annual convention and said, "So what are we going to focus on next? Audio." The crowd barely responded and then listened quietly as Jobs described how moving music onto CDs and into MP3 players was becoming the latest music revolution. Apple was late to this party, but, as always, it was designing a cool and easy-to-use product, iTunes, that would make it easier for non-computer nerds to do this. Neat. The crowd politely applauded here and there.[12,13] But it hardly seemed as though Apple had found the product that would allow it to displace Microsoft as the world's dominant computer company. Other companies, including Microsoft, had products that let people burn CDs. Other companies had MP3 players.

But Apple had already laid the foundation that would enable it to surpass Microsoft back in 1984, when the Macintosh transformed Apple into the brand that produces easy-to-use computer products that helped people think differently. Soon after, Apple introduced the iPod, which quickly became the market leader in the portable music player category. Then in 2003, Jobs introduced the iTunes Music Store. The major record producers, who saw their own business model crumbling thanks to illegal fire sharing, saw this as a lifeline and negotiated agreements with Apple. The day of the announcement, Jobs told the world that users already could download 200,000 songs for 99 cents apiece. For consumers, it was very relevant and very different. Unlike subscription-based internet services, the store enabled people to purchase songs that they could keep without having to pay subscriber fees. Unlike stealing from illegal download sites, it was fast and reliable and honest.[14] For content creators, it did nothing less than save the industry.

Then in 2007, Jobs introduced the iPhone, which was unlike any phone that had ever existed. In fact, it was so different that consumers might have been scared away by all those icons and apps had they not already trusted that the Apple brand is always easy to use. It revolutionized the cell phone industry. The company then introduced the iPod

Touch – basically an iPhone that doesn't make phone calls. In 2010, Apple introduced the iPad. It now dominates the tablet industry and threatens to make laptops a niche product.

In all of these products except the iPod Touch, Apple wasn't the first to market. Other companies have produced music players. Sony, was the brand associated with that category for years with its Walkman. Apple wasn't the first to make a smartphone. Research In Motion already had a healthy lead in that segment with its Blackberry. It wasn't the first to produce a tablet. Those had been floating around for years, unable to find a toehold. But only Apple was able to change all three market segments – because they were great products, of course, but also because of the brand. Music consumers and record labels gave the iTunes Music Store a chance because they trusted Apple. Smartphone buyers bought the iPhone because they knew it would be easy to use even though it looked hard. And people bought iPads because they knew they would be useful because Apple doesn't make anything that isn't.

For years, Microsoft had the better business model, the dominant market position, and the most money, but Apple had the better brand. Now look who's in front. Microsoft has tried to follow Apple, just as Windows had been a copy of Mac's operating system. All of its products – the Zune music player, the Windows Phone, the tablets that would compete with iPads – so far have failed to come close to eclipsing Apple. That's because, for consumers, Microsoft is the company that produces Windows and Office. It doesn't make phones and tablets. Apple can produce whatever it wants because it doesn't sell a product. It sells the ability to think differently. The result? In April 2010, Apple's market capitalization topped Microsoft's.[15] For a time in 2011, it was the world's largest publicly traded company. As of November 2011, it had $82 billion in cash on hand.[16]

Now Apple faces some new, unfamiliar branding challenges. The death of Steve Jobs will have an enormous impact on the company despite Apple's assurances that it won't. Jobs, of course, was the company's founder, visionary, master salesman and drill sergeant. Just as important, he was a central part of the company's brand. He wasn't just a rock star; he was the face of a company that is based on having a face. Another challenge facing the company is that it no longer can be the underdog for people who want to be the rebels, troublemakers and ones who see things differently. In fact, now it's the company that other underdogs will be branding as Big Brother. In fact, Samsung did just that in its 2012 Super Bowl ad featuring Apple users in front of an Apple store confronted with the upstart Samsung Galaxy Note. "I don't know what I believe in anymore," one young Apple enthusiast says while looking at Samsung's newer and supposedly better smartphone. How pathetic – he's lost his tribe, Samsung is saying. Now come join ours.

With its omnipresence, Apple is becoming what it once advertised against. Before it was barely relevant but very different. Can it remain different now that it is very relevant? Can it remain Apple at the same time it is becoming Microsoft? That's the challenge facing the company as it moves forward.

- 4 -

The Attention Economy

Traditional advertising involves one-way communication: The advertiser speaks and hopes potential customers are listening. It is based on an interruptive model, where advertisers interrupt the audience while they are consuming other content. The audience accepts that interruption out of habit and also because, one, it often is useful and sometimes entertaining, and two, the audience understands that advertising enables the content to be provided for free (television and radio) or at a reduced price (print). Who, after all, would want to pay money to watch "Three's Company"? Other forms of advertising, such as billboards and product placements in movies and television shows, also employ the interruptive model.

Unfortunately, no one can know if it actually works. Content providers can quote Nielsen ratings or subscription numbers, but they can't tell an advertiser how many people saw their advertisement versus how many went to the bathroom during the commercial or skipped over it with their digital video recorder. While overall brand awareness can be measured, it's impossible to pinpoint how many actual sales result from a particular advertisement. Branders can only shotgun their message to a very broad audience, such as those watching a television sitcom or reading a newspaper, or they can target their message to a specific audience that is likely to be interested in their products, such as the readers of Popular Mechanics or Vogue magazine. But they don't know if the person who wants to buy a hammer actually is looking at their ad for a hammer. And of course, all of this is tremendously expensive.

When the World Wide Web started becoming truly worldwide, content providers tried to follow that same interruptive model. Websites were glorified electronic marketing brochures. Content providers tried to make money using pop-up banner ads. News providers migrated their print model to the internet and offered their services at no cost with ads on the side of the screen. They lost money as well as print subscribers, who understandably asked why they should buy the cow when they could get the milk for free.

But in the past few years, advertisers have begun to figure this internet thing out – by targeting their messages to the right customers, and by paying for only those messages that accomplish their purpose. As we'll discuss in the next chapter, using mathematical algorithms, marketers can use your browsing history and online and offline purchases to target their advertising. If you buy tools, you're likely to see an ad for hammers. In fact, if you're looking to buy a hammer, they may know that, too. Meanwhile, unlike in traditional advertising, branders can pay only for the ads that they know actually work. The internet features two payment models, cost-per-mile (CPM) and performance. The CPM model charges branders each time their ad appears on a viewer's screen. It's interruptive like traditional advertising, and no one knows whether users noticed the ad or ignored it. Performance pricing, on the other hand, charges advertisers only for those ads that actually achieve an agreed upon purpose – a click, a lead, even a sale.

Not surprisingly, advertisers are spending more and more of their ad dollars on the internet, and they are spending more and more of that on the performance model. In 2011, sellers spent $31.7 billion on internet advertising, according to the Interactive Advertising Bureau. That's $5 billion more than the numbers reported in 2010. In 2002, the total number of ad dollars spent online was only $6 billion. Branders now spend more money on internet advertising than they do on cable television. In fact, the only medium where advertisers are spending more money is broadcast television, where they spent $38.5 billion in 2011. Meanwhile, the performance model is becoming the payment model of choice. Back in 2005 – and isn't it amazing that we can refer to 2005 as "back" – 46 percent of internet ad dollars was spent using the interruptive CPM model while 41 percent used the performance model. During the following seven years, the performance model has steadily risen to 64 percent, while CPM advertising has fallen to 32 percent. Advertisers, not surprisingly, want results, and performance-based internet advertising can guarantee them.

Still, this is a book about branding, not advertising, and branding is about more than just sales, although sales are the ultimate goal. Branding is about building relationships, and there is no better way to do that than social media – Facebook, Twitter, YouTube, etc. By August of this year, Facebook is expected to reach one billion active users who log in once a month.[1] In 2011, when it "only" had 700 million users, Time magazine asserted, "If the website were granted terra firma, it would be the world's third largest country by population, two-thirds bigger than the U.S."[2] Twitter announced in September 2011 that it had reached 100 million active users – also defined as those who log in at least once a month.[3] YouTube has hundreds of millions of users, according to its website.

Small wonder, then, that branders are spending big bucks here. Facebook earned $3.1 billion in ad revenue in 2011, and that number is expected to rise.[4] Twitter is expected to earn $226 million in ad revenues in 2012, an increase of 83 percent over what it earned in 2011.[5] Online news sources now bring in more revenues than print newspapers, which makes sense considering the increasing role social media is playing in reporting and in some cases making news. Politicians now make major announcements on Twitter. News of the death of Osama bin Laden was "broken" by a nearby Pakistani who, not knowing what actually was happening, tweeted his complaints about all the noise the helicopter was making. Meanwhile, social media was a vital tool throughout the recent Arab Spring. The world learned of the death of Neda Agha-Soltan, a student shot by Iranian security forces, and confirmed the death of Libyan dictator Muammar Gaddafi through videos posted online.

Social media offers an entirely new way of interacting with customers. Instead of giving a 30-second presentation that often is ignored – or, with digital video recorders, skipped over – advertisers can have a conversation. Through Facebook, Twitter and other sites, advertisers can listen or at least pretend to listen, and that's a powerful and necessary dynamic in a country that less and less wants to be preached at. Remember how people want to be a part of a tribe? Now brands can invite them around the fire.[6]

What a wonderful tool, and it's available to just about anyone – cheaply, even freely.

There's just one problem: It's available to just about anyone – cheaply, even freely.

If you're a social media user, then you know what I'm talking about. Facebook and Twitter are often just walls of sound and fury, signifying little, to paraphrase Shakespeare. YouTube claims that nearly eight years' worth of content are uploaded every day.

An online world is being created where so many are talking that it's hard to be heard. It's like instead of people sitting in church and listening to the preacher, everyone in the congregation has been handed a megaphone and told to yell as loudly and as often as they want. In 2010, of the more than 600,000 branded pages monitored by Facebook, only 57,000 had more than 1,000 fans. Starbucks was second with 3.7 million, while Coke was third with 3.5 million. Republicans need to pay attention to who was first – Barack Obama, the master of online branding, with 6.5 million.[7]

It's gotten harder to attract eyeballs no matter how much money, power and prestige one has. Last time I checked, the official White House version of the 2012 State of the Union address had 58,915 views. A clip of my first "Red Eye" appearance on Fox News Channel had 913 views. Meanwhile, videos produced by amateurs go viral and attract millions of eyeballs. Sometimes it's understandable. It's hard to script something as memorable as the "JK Wedding Entrance Dance," the YouTube video where a wedding party joyfully danced down the wedding aisle that has attracted almost 75 million views. It's hard to produce anything funnier than "David at the Dentist," where a drugged up seven-year-old's confused question, "Is this real life?" has attracted more than 110 million views. But the official version of Rebecca Black's awful "Friday" video has almost 29 million views, and frankly, no one knows why.

We are seeing a change not just in the advertising model but maybe in the entire economy. Michael Goldhaber, a former theoretical physicist, described in a 1997 speech and in a 1997 article in "Wired" magazine that Americans were watching an economic shift as fundamental as when capitalism replaced feudalism before the American Revolution. Traditional economies, he wrote and said, have been based on the production of tangible goods where the supply usually didn't meet demand. That made life hard for the human species, but it fit well with economic models that said that an economy is based on scarcity because scarcity determines what is valuable. In the past few decades, industrialized economies have turned that axiom on its head. Now in the developed world, manufacturers and farmers can produce more than what is needed. And internet content providers produce WAY more than what is needed.

The World Wide Web is often referred to as an "information economy," but Goldhaber said that's not correct. Instead, he said, it is an attention economy. Remember, economies are based on scarcity, and if there is anything that is not scarce these days, it's information. There's a glut of it, and if that's all you have to sell, you can't charge much for it. In fact, you're probably better off giving it away because it so easily can be shared anyway. What's really valuable these days is attention. Demand for that is increasing while the supply remains constant – each person only has 24 hours a day. Information is on the wrong side of the supply and demand equation, while attention is on the right side. In fact, attention is a form of wealth, a gift that keeps on giving because if I have your attention today, there's a good chance I can get it tomorrow. According to Goldhaber, the future belongs to those who are able to attract attention, which is why Paris Hilton can charge $200,000 for dropping into a party even though there are many pretty rich girls in the world.[8,9]

In the attention economy, different not only is good, it is necessary because people won't pay attention if there is no reason to look. Whereas the previous tangible goods economy valued standardization through mass production of identical items, the attention economy values creativity – videos of a bride and groom looking happy instead of stressed on their wedding day, and a high-as-a-kite kid saying goofy things to his dad from the back seat of their car after a visit to the dentist. In 2006, AT&T spent in the neighborhood of a billion dollars on its "Your World. Delivered." branding campaign. It achieved little, in part because it's still just the same phone company. What's to see?[10] Recent history offers many examples of independent candidates who ran for some office, achieved little and were forgotten. Ross Perot did the same but won 19 percent of the presidential vote in 1992. Why? Because he was folksy and funny, and because he offered a message about the future of the country. He was different, and he got our attention.

Goldhaber said a key part of this transaction is what he called "illusory attention," or the false sense we get that others are paying attention to us when in fact they are not. Goldhaber could not have known the exact form this would take when he was making his assertions in 1997. At the time he wrote that article, "Twitter" was the sound that birds make, but there's no better example of illusory attention. As of April 23, 2012, Paris Hilton had 6.9 million Twitter followers, all of them thinking on some level that she and they were having a conversation. According to her Twitter page, she was following 3,601.

I think you can see where I am going with this. (And notice that I use the words "I" and "you" as if we are having a conversation. We're not; you are paying attention to me.) Today's economy requires companies, politicians and celebrities to do something different than just advertising because advertising requires us to pay attention first. There has to be a reason for consumers to take their eyes off the highway, ignore the other billboards and radio ads (and emails and tweets) vying for their attention, and look in a certain direction. Branding through online media does that. It says, if you look over here, there will be something to see.

The implications of this power shift are enormous for branders. In the past it was about reaching the most consumers possible with a tightly controlled message. Now it's about connecting with a community that will produce its own message that can't be controlled. Instead of interrupting consumers with ads, branders must attract consumers who choose to go looking for them. Instead of barging into consumers' homes, they must inspire consumers to seek them out and invite them in. Instead of blasting a passive public with a barrage of advertising, they must develop individual relationships with their customers, particularly those with influence and large groups of Facebook friends and Twitter followers. Word of mouth has always been the most powerful, and most difficult to control, medium. In the online world, average Americans now have very large mouths capable of instantaneously sharing a lot of words. In this environment, effective public relations is becoming as important as effective marketing; in fact, the two are becoming intertwined. Instead of the PR side sending out press releases while the marketing side produces television commercials, the two communications arms must work together to tell their companies' stories.

Meanwhile, marketers must live in fear that millions of dollars spent on branding can be undone in an instant – or however long it takes to say, "I'm going to take my talents to South Beach and join the Miami Heat." Prior to July 8, 2010, LeBron James' brand was impeccable. His basketball talents were so extraordinary that, when he was still a junior at Akron's St. Vincent-St. Mary High, Sports Illustrated ran a cover story calling him "The Chosen One" and touting him as the next Michael Jordan. When he graduated high school, he was the first pick of the woeful Cleveland Cavaliers just 40 miles up Interstate 77. He instantly became an NBA star. In his seven years, he won two Most Valuable Player awards and took one of pro sports' least successful franchises to the NBA finals. In 2007, he yukked it up co-hosting ESPN's ESPYS award show. He was a fun guy who liked people, and the public liked him. In 2008, he helped the U.S. basketball team reclaim the gold medal in the Olympics.

Then in 2010 the story shifted as he entered free agency. Would he stay at home in blue collar Cleveland, or would he go elsewhere – the bright lights of New York City, perhaps? The media hype machine was running at full throttle, and James played it up by announcing his decision not through a press conference but via an hour long ESPN special that had the entire sports world's attention. "I'm going to take my talents to South Beach" meant he was leaving poor, downtrodden Cleveland to play in glitzy Miami along with fellow Olympians Dwyane Wade and Chris Bosh. The Cavaliers didn't even know what he was going to do until a member of his entourage phoned the team as the show was starting. The next night, the three superstars appeared in an over-the-top pyrotechnic celebration in Miami in which James predicted "not two, not three, not four, not five, not six, not seven" championships.

The whole thing – the decision to leave Cleveland, the collusion with his fellow superstars to stack the deck in their favor, the hour long special, which no athlete had ever done, the expectation of winning eight championships when he had yet to win one – turned James' brand on its head. Moments after his announcement, ESPN showed him footage of his jersey being burned in Cleveland. It seemed to take him by surprise. The entire country took Cleveland's side, which may have been a first. He went from beloved to hated and from hero to villain. The nationwide response was so vitriolic that Nike released a commercial with a sometimes forlorn, sometimes defiant James asking viewers "What should I do?" The Miami Heat became the NBA's bad guys, a role

James couldn't embrace. His feelings were hurt. The happy-go-lucky kid just playing his favorite game became a joyless, grim, burdened superstar and the object of fans' derision. From a branding standpoint, the only redeeming quality of his first season was that he didn't win the championship. That would have made him a permanent villain. During his second season, James did lead the Heat to a championship, and his gutsy play won – or re-won – him a lot of fans. His story went from being one of a pampered millionaire to one of redemption in the face of adversity. He hasn't returned to his former status as one of America's most beloved athletes, but he's definitely earned himself a new, and much better, brand.

LeBron James was rebranded thanks to 20th century technology – a cable television sports show produced professionally that was seen by millions and replayed for millions more. Today, companies know they can be rebranded by a single amateur video that goes viral. Instead of living in fear that "60 Minutes" is going to walk through the door, companies must live in fear of 20-somethings with iPhones. A 21-second clip of a FedEx deliveryman carelessly tossing a computer monitor had attracted 8.7 million YouTube views as of April 20, 2012, and forced the company into damage control. Worse was the 2009 video where a Domino's employee filmed her coworker seasoning sandwiches with his snot, sticking a piece of cheese that was in his nose onto a piece of bread, and passing gas above the food. "In about five minutes, it'll be sent out on delivery where somebody will be eating these, yes, eating them, and little did they know that cheese was in his nose and that there was some lethal gas that ended up on their salami. Now that's how we roll at Domino's," the female employee who filmed the scene narrated.[11] That, obviously, is a horrendous branding message. Domino's at first tried to ignore the problem, hoping it would go away. It wasn't going to go away. The video quickly had more than a million views. Soon it occupied five of the 12 results on the first page of a Google search for "Dominos." The company's quality perception went from positive to negative in the research firm YouGov's daily online surveys.[12,13] The two employees both were arrested and ended up serving suspended jail sentences.

The two incidents also showed how the online community could be helpful to companies like Domino's and FedEx. A Domino's spokesperson learned from a blogger and commenters of the video's existence as well as the location of the store where the incident occurred. FedEx responded to its embarrassing incident with tweets and a thoughtful blog post titled "Absolutely, Positively Unacceptable" that featuring a video and a written apology from a FedEx executive. That was an environment that it could control and one that was far more forgiving than if the executive had stood before a bank of microphones answering hostile questions from reporters.[14]

In fact, what the attention economy taketh away, it also can giveth. True, few would ever have known about that FedEx deliveryman a few years ago. On the other hand, there is now so much vying for Americans' attention that it doesn't take much to cause us to look the other way. Earlier this year, a pilot for JetBue flipped out and had to be locked out of the cockpit by the co-pilot and then restrained by the passengers. Parts of the incident were recorded by passengers with cell phones – something that wouldn't have happened a few years ago – and it was big news for a day or two. But executives responded, Americans' attention turned elsewhere, and the company sustained little damage from an incident that might have been far more damaging had it been discovered and reported by Walter Cronkite in the 1970s.

Companies' brands can be harmed by more than just a few wayward employees. Now the entire culture can be held accountable. Apple's brand recently lost a little of its shine when the New York Times published articles about working conditions at its Chinese factories. In a 2009 speech, Simon Clift, chief marketing officer of Unilever, warned that consumers can define a brand despite marketers' best efforts to do it themselves, so companies will find it harder to cover up acts of social irresponsibility with more marketing. "You may want to talk about sport and just doing it, and the consumer raises the uncomfortable question of sweatshops," he said.[15]

But companies that try to inoculate themselves from bad publicity by doing good deeds face a potential minefield. For example, what to some consumers is an admirable policy of tolerance against homosexuals is to others an attack on traditional values. What to some is a commitment to the environment is to others a pandering concession to greenies.

At the very least, companies and organizations shouldn't step their brands into dog poop on purpose when it comes to social issues, which is exactly what the Susan G. Komen Breast Cancer Foundation did. Until 2012, the Komen Foundation was universally beloved as an effective breast cancer-fighting organization. The foundation's Race for the Cure annually attracts millions of runners, many of them breast cancer survivors, in separate events across the county. As the women run, their men cheer them on. Who could not love that?

Now, a lot of people don't.

The Komen Foundation has inexplicably made a series of horrific branding decisions, starting with funding Planned Parenthood, one of the country's most polarizing organizations. Why the foundation couldn't find anyone else to offer breast cancer screening services is beyond me. When Congress planned to investigate whether any federal money was being used to pay for abortions, the foundation decided to stop giving money to Planned Parenthood. That caused a huge stink among pro-choice supporters and their allies in the media, so the foundation reversed itself. Now pro-lifers, many of whom hadn't been aware of the funding until the controversy began, were really mad.

The Komen Foundation expects to see a drop in revenue this year. More important is the long-term damage done to its brand – caused originally by its decision to fund Planned Parenthood in the first place. A breast cancer charity getting itself mired into the abortion debate? Someone at the foundation should have said, "This does not fit our brand."

The same forces that are transforming our economy also are changing our political process. While politicians will continue to blanket the airwaves with advertising, they also increasingly are using the tools of the Web to build their communities and spread their messages. Those who understand it will surprise a lot of people who don't on Election Day. In 2008, the absolute champion of the attention economy used those tools to help him win a presidency for which he clearly wasn't qualified.

We'll discuss this throughout the middle of the book, but first we'll spend one chapter talking about how branders are using technology to target their advertising in ways they never could before. In fact, they're using our own habits to brand us. The very idea of privacy is being turned on its head. And as we'll see later, that's changing politics as well.

- 5 -

The Branding of You

You go to the iTunes store looking to buy the latest song by Coldplay when a box appears on your screen asking if you want to install the latest update. As always, you click "I accept" without reading what you are actually accepting. After all, you couldn't have used the service the first time otherwise.

Have you ever thought about what you just agreed to?

Apple's privacy policy authorizes the company to collect certain personal information, such as your contacts and credit card number, that the company says will allow it to improve its products, services, content and advertising. It also can collect what it calls "non-personal information," such as your occupation, zip code and time zone, that the company says is not directly associated with you. When you click on a link in an email to the Apple website, that's tracked, though the company does helpfully say, "If you prefer not to be tracked in this way, you should not click text or graphic links in the email messages." The policy allows the company to track where you are when you use any Apple device, though it says it does so anonymously. However, it can't make the same promise for third party providers, such as makers of iPhone apps. "Information collected by third parties, which may include such things as location data or contact details, is governed by their privacy practices. We encourage you to learn about the privacy practices of those third parties," the policy says, as if anybody is going to take the time to do that.[1] Actually, we probably should. After analyzing 300,000 free apps for the iPhone and for Google's Android system, the mobile security firm Lookout, Inc., determined many were stealing sensitive data such as contact lists and search histories off consumers' phones and sending them to advertisers.[2] The policy allows Apple to disclose personal information about you to the government if so required by law or if the company deems it appropriate for national security or law enforcement purposes.

There are limits to Apple's ability to reach into your life. You can disable cookies, which websites encode in your browser to enable them to recall your past activities on that site. If you do disable, you will lose some of the Apple site's functionality. The agreement also allows you to opt out of receiving targeted ads on your mobile devices, though it does point out that you will see the same number of ads, but they won't be based on your interests. The agreement declares that Apple does not knowingly collect personal information for children under 13 – which means that, for children who are 13, it does.

Welcome to the world of predictive analytics, a rapidly growing business sector that tracks consumer characteristics and behavior. It's based on a simple idea: If you can find out a person's tendencies, you can place them into groups, and once you understand that group, you can predict how its individuals will behave in the ways that matter to you. Enormous amounts of information about us (and people like us), are digitally extracted from various sources – sometimes with our permission, often without our knowledge – and then fed into sophisticated algorithms to group us into clusters. Those clusters are then used to guess how an individual will respond to certain marketing techniques. Then marketers can use that information to target their advertising and buying offers to us. In other words, if I want to sell you a hammer and I know what motivates people like you to buy hammers, then I'm about to take your money.

The technique started being developed in the 1960s but did not begin to hit its stride until the 1990s with the advent of powerful and easy to use statistical and database software. By 1998, the Gartner Group was predicting that half of all Fortune 500 companies would be using the technique by the year 2000.[3] It's a safe bet that a lot more than half the Fortune 500 companies are doing it now. They know who we are, and they know what we probably want to buy. And how? Through our Google searches and our Facebook posts. Through commercial adware we download onto our computers that records the websites we visit. Through the GPS tracking systems in our phones. Through each purchase that we make with a credit card or gift card, which is one reason why retailers try so hard to entice us to apply for them. Through online coupons, whose bar codes contain a lot of information about us and not just about the product. Through store and brand loyalty programs that collect information about our buying habits and preferences that is then used to convince us to be even more loyal. Through software that scans the cookies stored in our browsers to send us personalized offers for products we might want to buy based on the sites we have visited. All of that information is combined with our other characteristics – age, gender, race, educational background, income level. And then companies put their products in front of us at the times and in the ways that most likely will lead to a sale.

For marketers, predictive analytics is a particularly useful tool for a very simple reason: When asked about their preferences using traditional methods such as focus groups and polls, consumers don't tell the truth – either because they don't want to, or because they are unable to. Why? They don't know what they want, and they don't know why they want it. In the 2000s, branding expert Martin Lindstrom demonstrated that fact through a $7 million study using MRIs and steady-state typography to track rapid brain waves of 2,000 subjects in countries across the world. One neuroimaging study found that, with smokers, even the most direct of cigarette package warning labels lit up the nucleus accumbens, an area of the brain associated with desire. That's right – the labels that warn of all kinds of awful diseases and death associated with cigarette smoking made smokers want to smoke, even though the smokers themselves reported otherwise.[4]

The tools are becoming very sophisticated and effective. The analytical device Predicta allows companies to cluster consumers based on their online activities and then target their advertising to them, which is why you may notice that the ads on the sites you visit seem to fit you and your needs so well. If you copy and paste an article from a website, then a company using the analytics tool Tynt.com knows about it through a process known as "behavior sniffing."[5] In 2011, the Wall Street Journal reported that web sites such as MSN.com and Hulu.com had begun tracking online activities using supercookies that were perfectly legal and, as the story said, "almost impossible for computer users to detect" because they are stored in different places than regular cookies. Those supercookies can recreate user profiles even after the users have deleted regular cookies. Meanwhile, the technique known as "history stealing" allows sites to look into users' web browsing histories to see where else they have visited. That lets companies know if users have visited sites dealing with potentially very personal matters, such as menopause and erectile dysfunction.[6]

Predicting consumer behavior in the past has been an art. Now it's becoming a science. As Lindstrom explained in his book, "Brandwashed," an executive at Canadian Tire in 2002 discovered from credit card receipts that buyers of carbon monoxide monitors and furniture floor pads never missed payments, while those who bought cheap motor oil and chrome skull car accessories were likely to do so. Meanwhile, credit card companies have determined that people who log into their online accounts late at night must be anxious about their finances and might start missing payments.[7]

The retailer Target in particular has employed predictive analytics very effectively. In early 2012, the New York Times' Charles Duhigg wrote a fascinating news article and book, "The Power of Habit," which included a description about how that company uses data to increase shopper loyalty when the shopper is pregnant.

Duhigg asserted that habits are formed and reinforced through a three-step process: There's a cue followed by a routine followed by a reward. For a person to change their own habits takes deliberate action. For a corporation to barge into that loop takes more marketing dollars than many could afford. However, there are certain points in people's lives when routines are disrupted and habits and attitudes are changed much more easily than others.

One of those times is having a baby, but Target didn't want to wait until after its shoppers' babies were born, because by then it's no longer a secret and parents are getting hit with offers from all kinds of companies who want their money. Target wanted to reach them in the second trimester, when parents are preparing for this momentous change and already looking at the world in new ways. "We knew that if we could identify them in their second trimester, there's a good chance we could capture them for years," Andrew Pole, a Target statistician, told Duhigg. "As soon as we get them buying diapers from us, they're going to start buying everything else too."[8]

Through the years, Target had collected data on all of its custom-ers based on their credit card purchases, coupon use, refund mail-ins, etc. It also knew basic information such as their ages, incomes, family situations, and even what websites they frequented. And, it knew how it could trigger certain habits – for example, emailing a particular shop-per a coupon might be effective at getting her to buy something online. Starting with using its own baby shower registries, Target was able to find about 25 products – unscented lotion, vitamin supplements, cot-ton balls bought in bulk – that were good predictors that a woman who was buying them was pregnant. In fact, the company could come close to determining her due date. So, if the company could get those women in its stores during her second trimester of pregnancy by enticing her with good deals on those products, it might change her shopping habits permanently.

How effective was the model at predicting if a woman was preg-nant? According to Duhigg, about a year after Target implemented it, a Minnesota man angrily complained to his local Target manager face to face that the company was mailing his teenaged daughter coupons for baby-related items, which he found outrageous. The manager apol-ogized to the father and then called his home a few days later to say he was sorry again. This time, the father had a different attitude: He wanted to apologize. It turned out he had a talk with his daughter, and Target's predictive analytical techniques were right: She was pregnant.

Now that the company knew how to tell when a woman was preg-nant, it had to be careful how it used the information. Shoppers don't appreciate a corporation knowing they are expecting a baby before they have had a chance to tell their own parents. So the company started sending catalogs to shoppers it thought were pregnant featuring both baby- and nonbaby-related items. It worked, and sales increased.[9]

This kind of data mining occurs offline as well. The company Brickstream sells a variety of solutions that help retailers study traf-fic patterns in their stores. Basically, shoppers are tracked by video throughout the time they are in the building, though the company says the video is not stored. Retailers can tell where a customer browsed, where she shopped, how long she stayed in a certain location and where she went from there. According to its website, the company, which was founded in 2002, enjoyed a record year in 2011.[10] A London-based company, TNS Global, has been tracking shoppers since 2001 to better understand their buying habits. Its PathTracker technology used a radio frequency device attached to carts and baskets that measured the paths shoppers took throughout the store, allowing retailers to know where they walked, how fast, and where they slowed or stopped. If a product purchased at the checkout line didn't match that path, then the store knew that the customer had left the cart to retrieve it. Soon the company incorporated video observations of shoppers and even managed to convince some to volunteer to wear eye-tracking technology so retailers could tell what was capturing their attention.[11] Using all of that data, the company was able to create distribution maps showing that American shoppers follow a very predictable path once they enter a store: They turn right and start heading toward the back in a counterclockwise motion. This happened despite store managers' best efforts to make them do otherwise by placing popular products in out-of-the-way places. The founder, Herb Sorensen, Ph.D., determined that the best way to get shoppers spending was to put the products they need in front of them quickly so their buying momentum builds and they spend less time wandering around the store buying nothing. He wrote a book, "Inside the Mind of a Shopper," about the process and how retailers could benefit from it. Sorensen wrote that the history of retailing has gone through three phases. The first was an active one where a helpful shopkeeper came to his shoppers' aid. The second was a passive one where supermarkets simply stocked everything on the shelves and expected shoppers to hunt for what they wanted. Now, he wrote, retailers are entering a new active phase where data plays the role of shopkeeper and encourages buyers to purchase certain products.[12]

There's no escape from all of this, so don't bother trying. And it's happening to all of us. According to AVG, an internet security firm, 92 percent of American two-year-olds have a digital footprint, while seven percent of newborns have an email address and five percent have a social network profile.[13] One German politician used a court case to determine that his cell phone company had recorded his location 35,000 times in six months. In 2010, Google CEO Eric Schmidt told the Techonomy conference in Lake Tahoe that humanity now creates as much information in two days as it did from the beginning of civilization until 2003.[14]

Much of that information is about consumer behavior online. And if you're concerned about that, here's what Schmidt told CNBC's Maria Bartiromo: "If you have something that you don't want anyone to know, maybe you shouldn't be doing it in the first place" – an argument that should be made by mamas and pastors but not by the CEO of a corporation that knows an awful lot about our private lives. What if the searcher is legitimately monitoring the activities of his or her government? Chinese citizens, as we know, also are tracked online. Schmidt himself acknowledged in his next sentence how Google increases the ability of the government to tap into our lives by saying, "But if you really need that kind of privacy, the reality is that search engines, including Google, do retain this information for some time, and it's important, for example, that we are all subject in the United States to the Patriot Act. It is possible that that information could be made available to the authorities."[15]

In George Orwell's novel "1984," the protagonist, Winston Smith, lives in a world where the government tracks citizens' every move through two-way "telescreens" set up throughout the landscape, including in people's homes. The system is designed to control their thoughts and maintain their loyalty, and it works very well.

Today, there's an Orwellian quality to these companies and the government knowing so much about us. Indeed, in 2007, London's Daily Mail reported that 32 closed circuit television cameras had been installed within 200 yards of the flat where Orwell wrote "1984." The flat's rear windows were under constant surveillance from two cameras attached to traffic lights. Meanwhile, within that 200-yard radius were hundreds of other private, remote-controlled security cameras located in homes, shops and offices. In fact, according to the article, Britain had one closed circuit television camera for every 14 persons in the country and 20 percent of all such cameras globally. The average Brit was caught on camera 300 times a day.[16]

Information is power, and an imbalance now exists between how much information the government and large corporations have versus how much citizens and small enterprises have. A government that can track our every move can control dissent and limit debate. Moreover, there's something un-American about being "clustered." We are supposed to be a nation of individuals, not a bunch of animals grouped and tagged in the wild. Finally, this technology offers large companies yet another advantage over small businesses. It's already hard enough for your local hardware store to compete with the economies of scale advantage that multinational corporations have. Now these huge companies know more about us than we know about ourselves. How can the mom and pops beat that?

On the other hand, let's not overstate the case. We're a long way from "1984." If the country feels less free than it did, say, 20 years ago, it's not primarily because of data mining or analytics. Instead, it's occurring because of old-fashioned government heavy-handedness, such as the individual health care mandate and airport screeners performing searches of old ladies and kids. In fact, if the government were more effective at data mining, it wouldn't need to resort to some of these measures. The world's most repressive regime, North Korea, is also a backwards one. It has maintained control for decades not through data mining but through a cult of personality, social pressures, systemwide poverty, and a heavy police and military presence.

In fact, when it comes to branding, all of this data in some ways is making us more free – for example, from the broadcast advertising model, which, as we have shown earlier in this book, isn't working as well as it once did. As we consumers have tuned out all of this marketing, advertisers have responded by turning up the volume in a vain attempt to get our attention. Because they haven't known who we are or what we want, they have had to stand on the rooftops and yell at all of us – unceasingly. Certainly, "1984" was a chilling fictional vision of the future, but so was the movie "Blade Runner," where advertisements ran in a loop on enormous billboards while marketing messages blasted across the sky. Now we're simply receiving ads for products we would like to buy on our desktop screens and phones. Is that so bad?

All of this data, when used correctly, enables us to improve our lives in real and measurable ways. The world is becoming so incredibly fast and complicated that systems must be designed to organize it. For example, the tools for interpreting consumer data help Walmart and Target put the right products on the right shelves, creating a more efficient economy that produces only what people want to buy.

Finally, as stated in the last chapter, these tools also enable average people to hold the powerful accountable. How did I find Eric Schmidt's comments to Maria Bartiromo? I googled them.

I started this chapter by making Apple the bad guy. That's not fair. Even in the midst of that privacy policy, the company took an opportunity to defend itself:

"Our goal in these cases is to make your experience with Apple more convenient and personal. For example, knowing your first name lets us welcome you the next time you visit the Apple Online Store. Knowing your country and language – and if you are an educator, your school – helps us provide a customized and more useful shopping experience. Knowing someone using your computer or device has shopped for a certain product or used a particular service helps us make our advertising and email communications more relevant to your interests. And knowing your contact information, product serial numbers, and information about your computer or device helps us register your products, personalize your operating system, set up your iCloud service, and provide you with better customer service."[17]

All of that is true, even laudable. I don't want to re-enter my contact information and credit card number every time I buy a song. I like being greeted on Amazon.com with a list of books that match my interests and on iTunes by songs I would like to hear. I think it's better for me and the economy when the advertising I see is advertising I need.

As long as it stops here, I'm fine with it. But if it goes much further, I'll be worried.

Anyway, some employee at Apple worked hard to craft that paragraph. I thought somebody ought to read it!

- 6 -

Giuliani, Obama, and Susan Boyle

Congressional campaigns don't begin the moment a candidate stands behind a podium and announces a run for office because he or she really believes in a set of principles. Most are born months or years earlier in back rooms and corner offices. That's also where they die. You want to get elected to Congress? You've got to impress people who can write checks and who have contacts and who can make things happen. It's a dance, really, between candidates and us political professionals. Either a potential candidate seeks us out, or we seek him or her out. Early in the process, candidates make contact with three types of individuals: a campaign consultant (a Karl Rove-type), a pollster (like Frank Luntz) and a fundraiser like me. We're looking for two things. First, do we agree enough with their political philosophy that we can live with them? And second, can they win? And more and more, the answer to that second question is based not only on impressive resumes and lifetimes of achievement but on whether that candidate either already has a good brand or can be branded. If they can win, we'll take them. If not, we won't. If we don't, it's going to be very hard – not impossible, but very hard – for that candidate to have much of a chance of winning in November.

Meanwhile, outside political groups play a major role in branding a candidate. Woe be unto Democrats who get on the wrong side of MoveOn.org. In the South, no candidate wants to be branded as anti-gun by the National Rifle Association. And when it comes to Republicans, if you want to make it out of a primary, it's best to have the support of the Club for Growth.

Founded in 1999, the Club for Growth is a political organization with very deep pockets that supports lower taxes and smaller government. When it backs a candidate, it does so generously, and it will not support a moderate based on political expediency. It usually wins, so candidates have learned to come knocking on the door early in the election season asking for its support. That interview goes a long way in determining who gets the endorsement. The board of directors and staff sit around tables looking at cards determining which candidates to support. And then the money starts flooding in. In my home state of Arkansas' Fourth District, the Club for Growth decided to support Tom Cotton, a handsome, unmarried Harvard Law School graduate and veteran infantry officer of the wars in Iraq and Afghanistan. In other words, he has a perfect brand. When Cotton started the campaign, he badly trailed his primary opponent, Beth Anne Rankin, a former Miss Arkansas who had run unsuccessfully for the seat two years earlier. Then Club for Growth money started rolling into Cotton's campaign coffers by the tens of thousands each week. She tried to make an issue of the fact that so much of his money was coming from out of state while hers was homegrown, and it earned her a little free press compared to the barrage of television commercials he was able to air. He won easily.

Cotton had a great brand as a veteran and an attorney willing to take a significant pay cut to serve in Congress, but Rankin had better name identification. But Cotton had another brand that proved more important: He was the Club for Growth candidate. That stamp of approval was a signal that he could be trusted to support lower taxes and smaller government. More importantly, it was a signal to donors where the race was headed. I've worked with candidates who have been on the receiving end of the Club for Growth's endorsement, and they were thrilled. I can only imagine the sinking feeling when a campaign hears that the Club has endorsed the opposition. Donors much prefer giving money to winners than losers, and once they see that Club for Growth brand on one candidate, it scares them from the others. Momentum builds. Once one candidate opens up a fundraising lead, he or she begins looking like a winner, and more donors jump on the bandwagon.

It's not just the candidates that are branded but also the campaigns themselves through a process called research-based communications. Issues are polled and studied extensively to discover which ones are the most important and to what voters. Through a technique known as microtargeting, which we'll discuss later, campaigns learn how to tailor their message to individual voters based on their demographic traits, online histories and buying habits. Once they know the base issues, the campaigns know they must align their brands with the voters.[1] For example, a recent poll in Arkansas' Fourth District by Talk Business found that only six percent of Republican primary voters there were in favor of gay marriage.[2] There may be some Republican candidates in Arkansas who do support gay marriage for a variety of reasons, but they had better not make that argument in the campaign if they want to win. According to Terry Benham with Impact Management, a political firm in Arkansas, "If you're not branding with the public, then you're basically selling ex-lax® to someone looking for lunch."

Benham, with whom I co-founded Impact Management along with our partner, Richard Bearden, has been working with Republican Party candidates for 20 years. He's watched his state go from being perhaps the most Democratic in the union to one that is poised to flip to the Republicans this election cycle thanks largely to Obama, whose brand is truly terrible in Arkansas.

According to Benham, once the base issues are known, then the campaigns work to brand the race and contrast themselves with their opponents. For example, if one candidate is a 30-year incumbent and the other has 30 years of business experience, and they largely agree on the base issues, and the polls show that jobs and the economy are the voters' primary concerns, then the challenger will try to brand the campaign as being about who has the real work experience necessary to create jobs. In fact, the candidate who brands the race in a way that's favorable to himself or herself probably is going to win. "If 50 percent of America is worried about jobs and the economy, and you brand the race on national defense, you just lost," Benham said. "Well, you just lost if the other candidate brands it on jobs and the economy."[3]

A political candidate must send consistent and continuous branding signals just as a consumer products company must do. Television advertising, direct mail, social media – it all must look the same and have the same message lest the candidate dilute the brand and hurt his or her credibility.

That's a challenge in today's media-saturated environment, where the branding doesn't cease and a brief moment or single comment can rocket around the world within days – even hours. In 2006 – and this was when Facebook and YouTube were in their infancy – Sen. George Allen of Virginia was running for re-election and considered a potential presidential candidate when, during a speech to supporters, he referred to an Indian-American videotaping him for his opponent's campaign as "Macaca." Many interpreted that as a racial slur, which he denied being the case. Regardless, he lost the election. As will be described later, Obama said in 2008 while campaigning at a San Francisco fundraiser that Americans "cling to guns or religion or antipathy toward people who aren't like them or anti-immigrant sentiment or anti-trade sentiment as a way to explain their frustrations."[4] He probably thought he was talking to a bunch of San Franciscans who by and large would agree with that statement. But he wasn't. He was talking to the world. The comment quickly made it around the internet and forced him to explain (badly) what he meant. According to Benham, "There are no off the record comments anymore. ...The mic is always hot in politics."[5]

Sometimes a potentially great public servant can have a great brand, like Sen. Marco Rubio, the Florida Republican who is brilliant, handsome, conservative and Latino at a time when Republicans are trying to enhance their standing among that important voting bloc. And then sometimes, it's just the right person with the right look at the right time. In fact, politics is looking more and more like a nationally televised talent show such as "American Idol" or "America's Got Talent." The judges on those shows didn't get where they are just because they look good on television. American Idol's Simon Cowell and Randy Jackson are both multi-millionaire music executives who know how to sell music. (Paula Abdul was there to offer eye candy and to soften the brand.) In those long lines of superstar wannabes, there are plenty of talented singers, but the shows are looking for someone they can brand, like girl next door Kelly Clarkson or all-American Carrie Underwood.

Or someone like Susan Boyle. If you have been anywhere near YouTube in the past three years, you know who she is. Boyle was a professional singer with a fabulous voice that was not going to get her out of her English cottage. By April 2009 she was 47 years old, single, dumpy and quirky, and there just wasn't much of a reason to look at her.

Then she became famous overnight because of a brief appearance on the show "Britain's Got Talent." The show's producers skillfully manipulated her audition into a seven-minute story of good, evil, triumph and redemption that aired three months later. Boyle's appearance started out as many do – with enough of a backstory to let viewers know they were about to witness either a rousing success or a complete failure, both of which would be equally compelling. Clownish music played as

Boyle, wearing an awful flesh-toned dress, ate a sandwich and admitted she had never been kissed. She strode onto a stage, temporarily forgot the word "cottages," and awkwardly flirted with Simon Cowell. It all happened in front of an audience that had seen some terrible acts earlier that night and didn't expect much from her.[6] How dare she think she could be as famous as Elaine Paige?! (Whoever that is.) The show's producers, of course, knew she could sing. Boyle confidently gave a thumbs up, the music began playing for "I Dreamed a Dream" (perfect for her brand), and she began to sing. The audience was stunned; apparently they had never seen a person who was not particularly beautiful be able to sing. They seemed to applaud her every note. Simon Cowell looked like he was in love, and he was – with the brand he saw in front of him that was about to make millions.

It wasn't just that a star was born two minutes into that seven-minute video. A brand was born as well. Susan Boyle is a beautiful singer, but there are many beautiful singers out there. What made Boyle stand out was her brand: the ugly duckling who stood on stage in her ugly dress while people laughed at her and, after a lifetime of failure, became a swan right before our eyes. She dreamed a dream. So do we. That was us standing up there. Simon Cowell became our boss, and the audience became everyone who ever put us down.

Boyle's first album, "I Dreamed a Dream," was the world's top seller that year, and she became one of the planet's most recognizable celebrities. She accomplished far more in that one audition than equally talented singers accomplish through years of touring and toil. She is far more famous than Elaine Paige. And all because of her brand.

Americans saw a similar dynamic in July 2004, when the Democrats were hosting their convention knowing they were nominating a candidate, John Kerry, with a terrible brand. Kerry was not a good fit for the Democrats. He was a rich guy who acted rich and wasn't named Kennedy. His votes and public statements sent all the wrong branding signals. A Vietnam War veteran, he seemed ambivalent about his service, and ambivalence is never good for the brand. He voted for the $87 billion for the Iraq War before he voted against it. What does that mean? George W. Bush never said anything like that. Kerry would have been better off becoming an anti-war crusader because of his experiences in Southeast Asia. Or he could have used those experiences to fashion a coherent policy of limited military force. Because he did neither, he had no story. And because he had no story, he had no brand.

So Kerry was not that great a presidential candidate. However, he might have been a good "American Idol" judge. After he secured the Democrats' presidential nomination, his team began preparing for the Democratic National Convention and came up with a short list of potential keynote speakers. During a two-day campaign swing through Illinois in April, he had been impressed with Obama, then a state senator who was running for the U.S. Senate. Obama was a rising star, emphasis on the "rising." Four years earlier, he hadn't been allowed inside the Democratic National Convention. Now he was the Democrats' nominee for an open Senate seat held by a retiring Republican. Democrats wanted that seat. Kerry thought Obama should become one of the Democrats' new faces.[7]

We all know what happened next. Obama strode to the podium and gave one heck of a speech. Remember back in chapter two when we talked about the importance of a brand being relevant and different? He was both. American politics had never seen a guy who looked like that, talked like that and had that kind of name. He spouted feel-good lines about there being no red states or blue states but a United States of America. What did he believe, and what were his qualifications? It didn't matter. The Democrats had fallen in love. A guy nobody had heard of was now a star because of one appearance. Just like Susan Boyle.

And like Boyle, Obama's newfound fame had occurred because of the right set of external factors. Had Boyle followed a couple of good acts by unattractive people – or a person with a better story, such as a war veteran or a person with a disability – she might have gone unnoticed. Had Kerry been a more interesting and inspiring candidate, the Democrats might have not have been in the mood for a new face. Had Kerry given Obama a different time slot – just off prime time, or the night before when he would have been competing for the audience's attention with Bill Clinton, Al Gore and Jimmy Carter, people might never have remembered that nice speech by that guy with the funny name. Obama didn't build a brand through years of achievement. He became one overnight.

Rudy Giuliani is just the opposite. His entire political career is a case study in the power and pitfalls of branding. Giuliani rose to prominence at the Department of Justice, where he became the associate attorney general, the agency's third highest-ranking position, and then became U.S. attorney for the Southern District of New York, where he gained a reputation as a tough-on-crime prosecutor. He narrowly lost his bid for mayor of New York City as a candidate of both the Republican and Liberal parties (yes, a future Republican presidential candidate ran as late as 1989 as a "Liberal" candidate), but then was elected in 1993.

As mayor, Giuliani led the effort in cleaning up New York's crime-ridden streets. When he was elected, the city was so dangerous that New Yorkers would post "no radio" signs in their car windows informing thieves that there was nothing worth stealing within. But Giuliani – and a lot of brave policemen and service-minded New Yorkers – set about to change that. They subscribed to the "broken windows" theory of community order, an idea first published by James Wilson and George Kelling in The Atlantic magazine that stated that crime arises from decay, that serious crime arises from minor violations, and that the way to start fighting crime was to fix a neighborhood's broken windows and to do something about the people who broke them. The result was an amazing turnaround. New York went from being a hellhole to being a safe city where people walked the streets without fear.[8,9] Crime was cut by two-thirds, and the welfare rolls were reduced by 691,000 people.[10] Giuliani, of course, got much of the credit, even though some of the work started before he took office. At the same time, many in academia, the media and elsewhere questioned methods employed by Giuliani and the NYPD, claiming they were racist and that they unfairly targeted the poor. A few high-profile cases of excessive use of force by police added fuel to that charge. Meanwhile, Giuliani's personal life was a mess. He was married 14 years to his second cousin and then had the marriage annulled. His second marriage to Donna Hanover also ended badly in 2000 after he marched in a St. Patrick's Day Parade with his then-mistress, Judith Nathan, and then announced his intention to separate from Hanover in a press conference.[11] Put it all together, and Giuliani had one weird brand: competent but tarnished.

But that changed in one day: September 11, 2011. For weeks, America's attention was riveted on its television screens. Giuliani arrived on the scene not long after the second plane struck the Twin Towers and almost was trapped inside his command center when the South Tower collapsed. While President Bush was still making his way back to Washington, Americans saw Giuliani walking along New York's smoky and chaotic streets surrounded by reporters, aides, fire department officials and others. He looked like a general arriving on the scene to tell everybody what to do. His press conference statement, "The number of

casualties will be more than any of us can bear, ultimately,"[12] summarized what all Americans were feeling. That day, he became the face not
only of New York City but of the entire country. "Tomorrow New York
is going to be here," he said. "And we're going to rebuild, and we're going
to be stronger than we were before. …. I want the people of New York
to be an example to the rest of the country, and the rest of the world,
that terrorism can't stop us."[13] During the next few months, Americans
watched as Giuliani attended hundreds of funerals of New York City
firefighters and police officers who died in the line of duty. One was Sgt.
Timothy Roy, an off-duty cop who had died trying to rescue survivors
at the World Trade Center. There Giuliani said to Roy's three children,
"He's with you – nobody can take him away from you. You have something lots of children don't have. You have the absolute, certain knowledge that your dad was a great man."[14] That year, Time magazine named
him its "Person of the Year" and called him "Mayor of the World."[15]

And that became Giuliani's new brand.

By 2007 Giuliani was the frontrunner for the 2008 Republican
presidential nomination. Even though six years had passed, his brand
was so impeccable that it counteracted his obvious problems fitting into
the GOP. While no one could question his national defense and law-
and-order credentials, his liberal social views, including his support for
abortion and gay rights as well as gun control, would have been toxic
for any other candidate. But no other candidate was the hero of September 11.

It was a huge honor when I was asked early in the campaign to
be one of Giuliani's national fundraisers. I handled 18 states, including
several in the South, which normally wouldn't support a northeastern
moderate from New York City who supported gay rights and gun control. Even if I really like a candidate, I won't work for him or her if I can't
raise money because I won't do them any good. Besides, I don't ask my
funders to support certain losers because then they may not donate to
my other candidates.

I was raising money for Giuliani – a lot of it, including in the South.
He had such a positive national brand after September 11 that I didn't
think he could lose. His numbers were high. The money was rolling in.
The candidate badly wanted to win. We were already picking out wall-
paper for our offices in the White House.

Unfortunately, the campaign wasn't worthy of the brand – or the
man. Giuliani's advisors knew he would be a tough sell in Iowa, the state

that holds the nation's first caucuses, which are dominated by social conservatives and Christian evangelicals. While those voters admired Giuliani because of September 11, it was reasonable to assume they weren't going to vote for a twice-divorced New York City mayor who supported abortion rights and gun control. Given that circumstance, campaigns like Giuliani's sometimes opt to skip the caucus altogether and focus their resources elsewhere, like New Hampshire, which holds the nation's first primary and which has a more libertarian outlook that would be far friendlier to him. Plus, New Hampshire is just a hop, skip and a jump over Vermont from New York.

But, convinced they couldn't win there, Giuliani and his political advisors decided to skip New Hampshire, too – and everything else until Florida on January 29 and the Super Tuesday states of February 5. Granted, Florida was the largest state up to that point and one with many retirees from New York, so it was the one he was most likely to win. But the result was a series of embarrassing defeats in the states where he didn't compete. On January 3, he captured only four percent of the delegates in Iowa, won by Arkansas Gov. Mike Huckabee, a social conservative. On January 5, he won no delegates in Wyoming's caucus. On January 8, he won only eight percent of the vote in New Hampshire, a state where he should have been competitive. Arizona Sen. John McCain won that one. On January 15, he won only three percent of the vote in Michigan, also a state not dominated by social conservatives. Former Massachusetts Gov. Mitt Romney won there. Similar results followed in Nevada, where Giuliani won only four percent of the vote, and South Carolina, where he won only two percent of the vote.

Throughout this process, the Giuliani campaign was reassuring its supporters, the media, and anyone else who would listen that this was all part of a grand plan that would come to fruition in Florida. We fundraisers didn't buy it. People give money to winners. Donors were asking a lot of questions. All we could do was lamely fall back on the Florida strategy excuse.

But something else was happening: Giuliani's campaign was beginning to look like a loser. It was hard to imagine a candidate winning three percent of the vote in Michigan and then turning around and being competitive against the Democrats in November. Meanwhile, Giuliani had built his brand on being America's mayor, the one who went to all the funerals and said the losses would be more than anyone could bear. Now he was picking and choosing states like this was all some kind of chess match? Who would he ignore as president? It almost looked like he didn't care. His supporters throughout the country – including in Florida – were disheartened. Meanwhile, McCain, Romney and Huckabee had become the frontrunners. On January 29, 2008, despite spending weeks there, Giuliani won only 15 percent of Florida's vote, picked up no delegates and barely beat the poorly funded Huckabee for third place. Only weeks removed from being the frontrunner, Giuliani was out of the race.

I am not the most objective source when it comes to my candidates. I believe in these people. I'd better, because I ask donors to fund them. But stepping back from it, I have no doubt that Giuliani would have beaten Obama in November. He was still America's mayor. He would have held on to the conservative base, which would have looked past his moderate social views because of September 11 and which would not have defected to Obama. Meanwhile, he could have picked up states, including New York, where Republicans normally aren't competitive. In fact, Giuliani was the only Republican candidate who could have beaten Obama in 2008.

Outside of politics, he remains forever branded the Hero of September 11. He's still one of my heroes. But if he ever runs for president again – and I would love to see him try – you can be certain he won't wait until Florida to get serious about it.

- 7 -

Branding the President

Raised poor on the frontier, Abraham Lincoln really wasn't that good a manual laborer and took pride in the fact that he had educated himself and become a successful Illinois lawyer. By 1860, his anti-slavery stance and ability to connect with people made him a potential Republican candidate for president. But still relatively unknown, he needed something more. Richard Oglesby, an Illinois politician, found it: two fence rails supposedly split by Lincoln and his cousin, John Hanks, 30 years prior. When Illinois Republicans met in May to nominate a presidential candidate, supporters carried in the two rails with a banner suspended beneath them reading, "Abraham Lincoln the Rail Candidate for President in 1860." Delegates responded with thunderous applause, and Lincoln easily won the state party vote on his way to the presidency.[1]

This was 1860. The country was inflamed by the question over slavery that, one year later, would split it in half. In fact, Lincoln's election was the tipping point that led to the Civil War. But those two split rails turned Lincoln into more than an anti-slavery candidate, of which there were plenty at the time. It turned him into a brand. This was marketing psychology's "halo effect" in action. By communicating one benefit of voting for Lincoln, that his physical strength had been forged through hard, humble work, Lincoln's campaign implied that his character would also be strong enough to lead the country through its present crisis. As the Smithsonian Institution's website puts it, "In that moment, Lincoln became a symbol of the self-made frontiersman and representative of honest, enterprising labor. Lincoln, the lawyer, became 'the railsplitter.' A life-sized painting was commissioned of a younger Lincoln, sleeves rolled up, shirt hanging open, splitting a rail as if he were Paul Bunyan."[2] The White House can be seen in the painting's background.

Today's, Lincoln's brand could hardly be better, except perhaps in pockets of Southern resistance. As Clare Boothe Luce said, "A great man is one sentence," and his is a doozy: Lincoln freed the slaves and preserved the Union. In reality, his story is much more complicated and nuanced. While he was opposed to slavery, he made numerous statements about African Americans that today would sound as if they had come from the Ku Klux Klan's grand wizard. For a long time, his prescription for correcting the historical wrong of slavery was to ship the slaves back to Africa. He made it clear in an 1862 letter, even as the Civil War was being fought, that he was willing to preserve the institution of slavery in order to preserve the Union. The Emancipation Proclamation, now revered as a founding document of freedom, was a largely political document that "freed" only the slaves in the Southern states, which, of course, at the time were in rebellion and not inclined to listen to him. Had Lincoln lived, he would have been responsible for stitching together a wounded nation, an ugly process that would have left him battered and diminished.

None of this lessens his place in American history; if anything, his personal growth when it comes to race relations enhances his heroism. It's merely to point out that Lincoln, considered by many to be the country's greatest president, is a brand. In reality, he was flawed like all of us. In history, he's become almost a messiah figure who entered office and rescued the nation only to have his innocent blood shed. While the Washington Monument is an abstract obelisk that inspires no one and the Jefferson Memorial is so far out of the way that you have to make a special trip to see it, the Lincoln Memorial has become almost a national church. People go there to restore their faith in the country, not to check it off their tourist to-do list. It's where Dr. Martin Luther King gave his "I Have a Dream" speech and where Glenn Beck held his Rally to Restore Honor. In life, Lincoln had a good brand, at least in the North. In death, it's the best in American history.

But he's far from the only president to have one. George Washington understood the importance of branding, though he wouldn't have called it that. He was not the most educated Founding Father; in fact, he had less formal education than did Lincoln, which is somewhat surprising because his brand suggests a more aristocratic upbringing. But he cultivated a rock solid character as well as a manner that engendered such trust that, despite all the great minds around him, he was the natural man to lead the Continental Army as well as serve as president of the Constitutional Convention. His signature atop the list of names endorsing the Constitution was a signal to skeptical Americans that the new government was worth pledging allegiance to. His brand was so spotless that the enormous egos who founded the United States unanimously elected him its first president. He is known as the father of our country for a reason: because he was.[3] It's a great brand.

Between Washington and Lincoln were other presidents who understood or at least benefitted from the power of branding. While Thomas Jefferson wrote the Declaration of Independence, James Madison is considered the father of the more important Constitution. Which one occupies the higher place in American history? Jefferson. He has a better brand. "Old Hickory" Andrew Jackson, the nation's seventh president, styled himself a man of the people and then lived up to that brand promise during his inauguration by throwing open the White House to the mob of Americans who had come to see him.

The election of 1840 may have marked the birth of purposeful political branding. William Henry Harrison, the Whigs' losing candidate of 1836, again was running for president at age 68. After four years of the inept Martin Van Buren, his party was eager for a victory, so it fashioned an image that would propel him to the White House. Born in relative affluence in Virginia, his campaign portrayed him as a "log cabin" candidate. Meanwhile, it resurrected the nearly forgotten Battle of Tippecanoe, led by Harrison 28 years earlier against the Shawnee Indians. Once John Tyler became his running mate, the campaign's slogan became "Tippecanoe and Tyler Too." When Democrats said Harrison would do nothing but drink hard cider, his own party took to calling him the "hard cider candidate." Harrison's empty campaign carried the day, but alas, he didn't spend much time in the White House. After giving a two-hour inaugural address on a cold March day, he developed pneumonia and died only one month into his first term.[4] That wasn't good for the brand.

Forty-four years later came an election that resembles today's mudslinging affairs. The campaign of 1884 pitted Democrat Grover Cleveland against Republican James Blaine, and both men's brands would suffer. Cleveland came under fire because he had hired a substitute to fight in his place during the Civil War. Blaine had been implicated in a financial scandal when he had run for president eight years earlier. It got worse. During the campaign, it came to light that Cleveland was having an affair with a Buffalo widow and may have fathered her child. To play up the scandal, Republicans chanted, "Ma, Ma, where's my Pa?" Then Blaine's campaign was struck a fatal blow when he sat quietly while a Protestant minister said, "We don't propose to leave our party and identify with the party whose antecedents are rum, Romanism, and rebellion." Blaine lost New York by 1,000 votes and, with it, the election.[5]

The early part of the 20th century would see the acceleration of political branding. Teddy Roosevelt's entire life was a brand, though one that was created honestly. He led the Rough Riders up San Juan Hill; he was a big game hunter; in his last presidential race, he gave a speech after being shot by a would-be assassin. The teddy bear was created in response to a hunting incident when Roosevelt refused to shoot an old bear his party had trapped for him because it wouldn't have been sporting. The incident, portrayed in a famous editorial cartoon, led to the creation of the bear as a child's toy and enhanced Roosevelt's reputation as a man of honor. Three presidents later was Calvin Coolidge, known today as much for his quiet demeanor as his conservative political philosophy. Today, his "Silent Cal" nickname enhances his conservative reputation because a man who was so frugal with his words must have been frugal with the taxpayers' money.

Herbert Hoover, on the other hand, had a terrible brand, and still does. Because he was in office when the Great Depression struck, the shanty towns of homeless people that sprang up were known as "Hoovervilles." There's no way that his policies in his one term were responsible for the worldwide collapse. In fact, he had been in office less than a year when the stock market crashed. He responded with relatively modest expanded public works spending while trying to keep the budget balanced. Meanwhile, his life before and after was marked by achievement. As head of the American Relief Administration, he helped feed millions of starving people in Europe and Russia. He was secretary of commerce under two presidents, Harding and Coolidge, before his election and was appointed to chair important commissions under two later presidents, Truman and Eisenhower. No matter. He was the Republican president who was in office when the Great Depression hit, and, unlike his successor, the Democrat Franklin Delano Roosevelt, he didn't respond by exploding the size and role of government. That has made it easy for historians and the media to brand him a failure.

Teddy Roosevelt, Coolidge and Hoover lived in an era before modern mass media played such a huge part in our national life, and yet branding was a part of their presidencies and now is part of their historical record. Franklin Roosevelt, on the other hand, came on the scene at the perfect time. Roosevelt understood the power of branding, though he probably didn't think of it as such at the time. Stricken with polio as a younger man, he was largely confined to a wheelchair, a condition he knew would make him unelectable – especially at a time when Americans needed to believe in a strong president. So he "walked" by leaning on a cane with one arm and on one of his sons with the other and twisting his hips back and forth to make his useless legs swing forward. Thanks to the limits of communications technology and the restraint shown by the political press, he was able to maintain the fiction that he could walk for many years. Meanwhile, he effectively used the marketing tools that were available to him, including his "fireside chats," which connected him with Americans via radio during those difficult years.

From that point forward, every American president has been a brand. The plain-spoken Truman was "Give 'em hell, Harry!" Dwight Eisenhower, hero of World War II, was the ultimate brand for his time. He campaigned under the slogan, "I like Ike," but he didn't even need that. There was no way the Democrats' candidate, the bookish Adlai Stevenson, was going to defeat the man who planned and executed the victory over Hitler.

His running mate, Richard "Tricky Dick" Nixon, on the other hand, had a different brand, and not a very good one. In 1952, soon after Eisenhower picked him as his running mate, Nixon became the subject of a New York Post report that he had a secret slush fund worth $18,235. His vice presidential campaign in peril, he responded with a nationally televised address to 60 million viewers on September 18, 1952, in which he denied ever receiving any personal gain from that fund.[6] Instead, he said, he had used it to defray the costs of his political activities rather than charging them to the taxpayers. Pivoting, he then told the television and radio audience that he would share with them his entire financial history, which he did, but what he really was doing was taking the opportunity to share his modest roots, remind Americans that he was a war veteran, and emphasize that he and his wife, Pat, were not wealthy. Pat, he said, did not wear a mink coat. She wore a "respectable Republican cloth coat." Memorably, he added that he did receive one gift after the election from a radio listener who had heard Pat mention that the family did not have a dog. "And believe it or not, the day before we left on this campaign trip we got a message from Union Station in Baltimore saying they had a package for us," he said. "We went down to get it. You know what it was? It was a little cocker spaniel dog in a crate that he had sent all the way from Texas, black and white, spotted, and our little girl Tricia, the six year old, named it 'Checkers.' And you know, the kids, like all kids, love the dog, and I just want to say this right now, that regardless of what they say about it, we're gonna keep it."[7]

This may be Nixon's most famous address aside from the one where he resigned from the presidency. It became known as "the Checkers speech" because, in memory, at least, the part about the little dog did more to enhance his brand than his entire explanation of his family's finances. No amount of paid advertising could have so effectively painted him as a husband, father, and middle class American. It saved his political career and his brand – for a time, anyway.

President John F. Kennedy introduced a new kind of brand to American politics. You may have heard the story of how his 1960 debate with Nixon turned on the fact that Kennedy looked good on camera while the unshaven Nixon did not, and that Kennedy won among those who watched the debate on television while Nixon won among those who listened to it on radio. But the branding went much deeper than that. Branding, in fact, was critical to a presidency that wasn't what it seemed. Americans were led to believe that their young president and his wife were living a "Camelot" existence in the White House. The truth was that Kennedy was recklessly unfaithful with all kinds of women. They were led to believe that he was a vigorous young leader. The truth was that he had been stricken with a variety of illnesses from age 13 on. In 1947, he was diagnosed with Addison's disease, an adrenal insufficiency that can result in death if untreated. By the time he was president, he was taking 10-12 medications a day.[8]

Future presidents would not be able to maintain such fictions. During the 1960s, Americans became more savvy and cynical. Kennedy's presidency was followed by the United States' escalating involvement in Vietnam – an effort led by a president, the uncouth insider Lyndon Baines Johnson, whose brand was ill-suited for the changing times.

And yet LBJ was able to win re-election in 1964 because he was able to use one of the most powerful branding tools of all: fear.

That year, Johnson faced one of the fathers of the modern conservative movement: Arizona Sen. Barry Goldwater. Goldwater didn't shy away from labels, declaring in his acceptance speech at the Republican National Convention that "Extremism in the defense of liberty is no vice." He did not apologize for his strong conservative stance, which included votes against the supposedly anti-poverty Economic Opportunity Act of 1964 and the Civil Rights Act of the same year. In a 1964 television interview, he said he would be willing to use nuclear weapons in Vietnam, which at that point still seemed winnable by other means. Plus, he just looked like a hard guy.

All of that made it easy for Johnson to brand him using our old friend the amygdala, the very powerful part of the brain that deals with fear. Remember how the amygdala is designed to override other parts of the brain, including logic, because we might not have time to think about why we need to run from the bear? Johnson's campaign turned Goldwater into the bear. His campaign unveiled an ad, which ran only once, that featured a little girl in a meadow counting (and miscounting) the petals of a daisy as birds chirped in the background. Suddenly, her face was frozen as a voice that could only come from a military officer began counting down from 10. The camera zoomed in on her and then cut to an exploding nuclear bomb as Johnson declared in a voiceover, "These are the stakes: To make a world in which all of God's children can live, or to go into the dark. We must either love each other, or we must die." In case the viewer didn't make the connection, a voiceover following the mushroom cloud implored viewers to "Vote for President Johnson on November 3. The stakes are too high for you to stay home."[9] The implication was that voting for Goldwater might result in a nuclear attack, while Johnson would never allow such a thing because of his great love for all of God's children.

The media environment in the last half of the 20th century would make branding one of the main ways that presidential candidates would win and lose elections. In 1967, Gov. George Romney, father of Mitt, was a Republican frontrunner for the 1968 nomination – until he was asked on television why he had changed his position on Vietnam. At the time, he was saying the United States shouldn't have gone to war. In 1965, he had expressed support for the effort after returning from a visit there. "Well, you know when I came back from Vietnam, I'd just had the greatest brainwashing that anybody can get ... not only by the generals but also by the diplomatic corps over there. They do a very thorough job," he responded.[10] The description of brainwashing was not meant literally, but a lot of people took it that way. He lost and is remembered for that line today. In 1972, reporters claimed that Sen. Edmund Muskie, a frontrunner for the Democratic presidential nomination, had shed tears while reacting to a newspaper publisher's attack on him and his wife while campaigning during a snowstorm in New Hampshire. It's still disputed whether he was actually crying, but it nevertheless branded him as too weak to be president. A couple of comical and highly publicized falls climbing up and down the stairs of Air Force One turned Gerald Ford, perhaps the nation's most athletic president ever, into the man who was too clumsy to hold the office. Chevy Chase's goofball impersonations of him on "Saturday Night Live" practically made him unelectable. Jimmy Carter, a peanut farmer with a paper-thin resume who had served only four years as governor of Georgia, won his party's nomination and then the presidency because he was able to brand himself the anti-Nixon with his accent and big grin. He just seemed like an honest, common man. It was a good brand, but not strong enough to withstand four years of his failed policies. In 1988, someone in the campaign of Democratic presidential nominee Michael Dukakis had the bright idea of filming him riding stiffly in an Army tank while wearing a coat and tie. The goal was to burnish his credentials as a potential commander-in-chief, but he could not have looked more awkward or out of place. The Republicans used the footage in their own ads to point out his soft defense positions. Dukakis also damaged his brand when he botched an answer to a hypothetical debate question about whether he would support the death penalty if his wife were raped and murdered. His passionless response explaining his opposition to the death penalty reinforced his brand as a robotic policy wonk. The man who beat him, President George H.W. Bush, later had his own branding problems. After he politely showed interest in a supermarket scanner during a visit to a supermarket trade show in 1992, the New York Times and his opponents made the leap that he had never seen such a gizmo in action. It reinforced the idea that he was out of touch with average Americans at a time when many were suffering in a bad economy. Worse from a branding standpoint was his compromise with Democrats in Congress to raise taxes after famously declaring, "Read my lips: No new taxes" during the campaign. The right wing never forgave him, and the public no longer could trust him. In 2004, former Vermont Gov. Howard Dean was one of the frontrunners for the Democratic presidential nomination until he lost the Iowa caucus, which was disappointing, and gave a wild-eyed concession speech before a cheering crowd of supporters that ended with what became known as the "Dean Scream." That was devastating. He looked like he was becoming unglued before the nation's eyes – certainly not a good brand for anyone who wanted to be president.

In their book, "The 22 Immutable Laws of Marketing," Jack Trout, president of the international marketing firm Trout & Partner, and Al Ries, chairman of Ries and Ries, listed their 15th law as "The Law of Candor: When you admit a negative, the prospect will give you a positive."[11] They explained that admitting a problem makes a company better able to connect with its customers because while customers may doubt a positive statement a company makes about itself, they always will believe a self-criticism. They listed Listerine as an example. When rival Scope began a marketing campaign based on the fact that it tasted better, Listerine responded by admitting a negative and describing its own product as, "The taste you hate twice a day." It worked because customers figured that a mouthwash that tasted like medicine must actually kill the germs that caused bad breath.[12] A more recent example is the Domino's Pizza ad campaign where the company touted its new recipes by very openly bashing its old ones – even showing footage of criticism by focus groups. Revenues increased five percent while earnings have risen 20 percent in the past year.[13]

The words "Bill Clinton" and "candor" typically aren't associated with each other, but in February 1992 Clinton followed the law of candor and reaped the benefits. That's when he and Hillary Clinton were televised sitting across from "60 Minutes" interviewer Steve Kroft shortly after the Super Bowl answering questions about a former Little Rock television reporter who had made a sudden name for herself by alleging during a news conference that she and Clinton had engaged in a 12-year affair.

Prior to late 1991, Clinton was known to the world mostly as the Arkansas governor who gave a long, rambling speech at the Democratic National Convention and then joked about it with Johnny Carson not long afterwards – a masterful use of the law of candor in itself. If he could joke about it, he must be OK. When he announced he was running for president, it didn't make that big of a splash. But as the campaign continued, Clinton was making inroads on a weak Democratic field – until Flowers made her allegation. Eight years earlier, allegations of infidelity had sunk the insurgent campaign of Sen. Gary Hart, and now they looked to be sinking Clinton. Largely unknown to voters until then, Clinton was being branded as 1992's Hart. And that's why he was on "60 Minutes" immediately after the Super Bowl talking about sleeping around on his wife.

It would have been a tough interview for anyone who had been less than faithful to their spouse. Asked about Flowers' charge that they had a 12-year affair, Clinton declared, "That allegation is false,"[14] without specifying if he was talking about the entire allegation or just one of the details. The affair? Or the 12 years? It didn't matter. He and Hillary looked like a loving couple who had worked through their earlier differences. They sat close together on a love seat while Kroft asked them questions most Americans would not dare ask another couple. Clinton did not specifically admit that he had been unfaithful during his marriage, but he made it clear enough that he had been. Pressed, he took the offensive. "I have acknowledged wrongdoing," he said. "I have acknowledged causing pain in my marriage. I have said things to you tonight and to the American people from the beginning that no American politician ever has. I think most Americans who are watching this tonight, they'll know what we're saying. They'll get it, and they'll feel that we have been more than candid. And I think what the press has to decide is, 'Are we going to engage in a game of 'gotcha?'"[15]

Clinton's performance, though at times shaky, didn't merely save his brand. It enhanced it. A politician many in Arkansas had long decided had trouble with the truth now looked like an honest, reformed husband with the dignity and restraint to avoid going into details about his marriage. Americans were left to wonder why the news media were making such a big deal of his past indiscretions if his apparently loving wife had come to terms with them. And by appearing after the Super Bowl at a time when few Americans were paying close attention to the campaign and had not yet heard of his opponents, Clinton solidified his status as the reformed frontrunner. If the election would be about whether or not Clinton was a good enough husband – well, apparently he was.

When he finished in second place in the New Hampshire primary, he branded himself "The Comeback Kid." The media bought it, relegating the candidate who actually won the primary, the far less sexy former Sen. Paul Tsongas, to second-tier status. Clinton would go on to win the Democratic nomination and the presidency. Later, he was able to survive more than one scandal involving a woman who was not his wife, in large part because Americans had come to accept that an occasional act of infidelity was part of the Clinton brand.

- 8 -

Branding Republicans vs. Democrats

More than 100 years ago, America's favorite homespun philosopher comic, Will Rogers, said, "I'm not a member of any organized political party. ... I'm a Democrat." He also said, "Democrats never agree on anything. That's why they're Democrats. If they agreed with each other, they would be Republicans."[1]

Those two statements explain a lot about why Republicans have occupied the White House 20 of the past 32 years. Because whether or not you agree with the GOP, there is little doubt that, since 1980, it has had a better brand than the Democrats.

Why? Let's start with this: The key to any successful branding effort is to reduce what your organization stands for to a brand driver, a message that is so simple and straightforward that it almost can't be misinterpreted.[2] That applies to any product in the marketplace, and politics is merely the marketplace of ideas.

In 1932, President Roosevelt proposed his "New Deal," and those two words, along with America's victory in World War II, defined his presidency and enabled the Democrats to remain in power for much of the next 50 years. FDR's basic assumptions – that government played society's primary role in addressing inequality and poverty – remained relatively unchallenged regardless of who was in the White House. The modern conservative movement, which did challenge those assumptions, and its association with the Republican Party did not begin to take shape until the 1964 election, when Barry Goldwater ran for president, but he won only 36 percent of the popular vote that year, and neither President Nixon nor President Ford governed as conservatives.

Reagan gave the Republicans their own compelling brand driver summarized in his first inaugural address: "In this present crisis, government is not the solution to our problem. Government is the problem." He has been called "The Great Communicator," but that was made possible because he was also "The Great Brander." In their book, "The 22 Immutable Laws of Marketing" – and we'll refer to this excellent and easy-to-read book several more times in this chapter – branding gurus Jack Trout and Al Ries wrote that the 14th law of marketing is "The Law of Attributes: For every attribute, there is an opposite, effective attribute."[3] In other words, if your competitor already owns a word or trait in the marketplace, you can succeed by owning the opposite one. Reagan understood that law. If Democrats were the party of big government, then Republicans were the opposite, and while Democrats would fumble to explain why government should manage our lives for us, Republicans could offer a simple eight-word brand driver: less government, lower taxes, strong defense, traditional values.

Reagan's ideas now are the standard of politics. Republican candidates may disagree about specific issues, but they cannot mess with that brand. Democrats, meanwhile, are playing catchup. In his State of the Union address in 1996, President Clinton stated, "The era of big government is over." Even President Obama gives Reagan credit for this sea change in American politics. While running for the Democratic Party nomination in 2008, he said, "I think it's fair to say the Republicans were the party of ideas for a pretty long chunk of time there over the last 10-15 years in the sense that they were challenging conventional wisdom."[4] He went on to say, "I think Ronald Reagan changed the trajectory of America in a way that Richard Nixon did not and in a way that Bill Clinton did not. He put us on a fundamentally different path because the country was ready for it. I think they felt like, you know, with all the excesses of the sixties and the seventies and government had grown and grown, but there wasn't much sense of accountability in terms of how it was operating. And I think, people just tapped, he tapped into what people were already feeling, which was we want clarity, we want optimism, we want, you know, a return to that sense of dynamism and, you know, entrepreneurship that had been missing."[5]

Reagan was successful because he was right, but he also was successful because he was first. Let's go back to "The 22 Immutable Laws of Marketing" and look at the third law, "The law of the mind," where Trout and Ries wrote that whoever is first in a category – not first to enter the marketplace, but first to enter the public's collective mind – can own the category. Advil, Tylenol, Hertz – all were first in the public mind in their categories (ibuprofen, acetaminophen, rental cars) and all remain first today. In fact, being first in a category is more important than being better. The two pointed out that Charles Lindbergh is a household name because he was the first person to fly solo across the Atlantic Ocean. Who was the second? Bert Hinkler, who flew faster and consumed less fuel but has been forgotten by history.[6] Roger Bannister is remembered in history as the first person to run a four-minute mile, considered at the time to be an almost impossible human achievement. For months, Bannister had been in a race to set the mark with the Australian runner John Landy. The two were coming closer and closer to setting the four-minute mark until finally Bannister accomplished the feat with a time of 3:59.4. Landy broke that record within a month – in other words, he was faster and better, at least for a time.[7] But he was not first, and that's why Bannister was Sports Illustrated's first Sportsman of the Year in 1954. Same goes for John Adams (second president) and Buzz Aldrin (second human to walk on the moon).

Reagan was the first candidate to personify the conservative movement at a time when Americans were ready for its message, and because of that, Republicans own "less government," "lower taxes," "strong defense," and "traditional values." His ownership of that brand enabled him to be forgiven when circumstances and his policies changed. After cutting taxes soon after entering office, Reagan later raised them, though not to previous levels. No matter; he still was branded as a tax-cutter. After urging Mr. Gorbachev to tear down the Berlin Wall, he went on to sign the Intermediate-Range Nuclear Forces Treaty reducing nuclear weapons. No problem; everyone knew he wasn't soft on defense. Those who called him the "Teflon president" because nothing stuck to him didn't understand what was really happening. It wasn't the Teflon. It was the brand.

The Reagan legacy for Republicans isn't just that they own "less government," but they also own words associated with that concept, like "self-reliance" and "independence." Similarly, by being the party of "strong defense," Republicans own "strength," "security" and even "patriotism." By being the party of "traditional values," Republicans speak to Americans' worries over the breakdown of the family and the coarsening of the culture.

Unfortunately, the market is only generous to a point, and then it gets stingy. In his book "Big Brands, Big Trouble," Trout wrote, "If you're known for one thing, the market will not give you another thing." He cited Xerox, which so dominated the personal copier industry that the company's name became both a verb ("Please xerox this") and an adjective ("Make a xerox copy"). Xerox tried to enter the personal computer market and even produced the first computer with a mouse and the kind of graphical interface today used by both Windows and Apple. The product went nowhere, in part because Xerox already had a brand – as a copier company. Instead, Trout wrote, Xerox should have approached the personal computer revolution by becoming the leader in that segment of the market where it already had built huge brand equity – the transfer of information onto paper, or printers. Now Xerox doesn't make computers and owns only a small part of the printer market.[8]

That same branding principle works against Republicans, who don't get much credit for enacting big government policies even when they want that credit. George W. Bush ran for president as a "compassionate conservative." In eight years, he expanded Medicare benefits, greatly expanded the federal government's role in education through No Child Left Behind, and created one of the great humanitarian programs in American history, PEPFAR, the President's Emergency Plan for AIDS Relief. PEPFAR was lauded by musician and anti-hunger crusader Bob Geldoff, who wrote in Time magazine, "The Bush regime has been divisive — but not in Africa. I read it has been incompetent — but not in Africa. It has created bitterness — but not here in Africa. Here, his administration has saved millions of lives."[9]

You would think that, given his record, liberals would love Bush, or at least love part of what he did. If a liberal had signed No Child Left Behind into law, the media would be calling for his head to be carved onto Mount Rushmore. But Bush's party wasn't the right one, and his brand wasn't the right kind. Bush fit into the Republican brand. He talked like a conservative. He looked like a conservative. And he cut taxes like a conservative. He did not cut spending like a conservative. But as we saw in the 2004 election, thanks to his brand, he didn't have to.

According to Ries and Trout, when two organizations are competing in marketing, there is only one move that can produce significant results. They compare it to the Allied D-Day invasion of Normandy, the point at which Adolf Hitler was most vulnerable. They call it the "Law of Singularity."[10]

I don't believe there is only one move that can produce results, but certainly everybody has an area of greatest weakness. That being the case, where is the Republicans' Normandy? Historically, the GOP has been "the party of the rich" or "the party of big business." Democrats could exploit that vulnerability at a time when income inequality is rising and the richest 400 Americans have as much wealth as the bottom 50 percent. In the debate over tax cuts, Democrats score points when the argument centers on the top rate, as Obama seems determined to make it, rather than on overall tax rates, where Republicans are stronger.

There are other weaknesses in the Republican brand. Being the party of less government can be awkward when so many of your own voters depend on Social Security and Medicare. Also, being the party of "traditional values" can be problematic when certain American values, such as support for gay marriage, are changing. Republicans should continue to be the party where social conservatives find a home because that large bloc of voters is not going to be at home with the Democrats. However, if the Republican brand becomes associated with intolerance, then an important part of the party's coalition – libertarians who believe in less government in both fiscal and social spheres – might find somewhere else to go, and young people might never give the party a chance.

Changes in American demographics perhaps spell the most trouble for Republicans, who unfairly have been branded by some as "the party of white people." Left unchanged, that potentially will be poisonous as the country becomes more diverse and as Caucasians become a minority. On one occasion as I waited backstage before a television appearance, Democratic strategist James Carville pointed his finger at me and said that, because of demographics, Democrats were headed to a 40-year majority. Indeed, he wrote a book making that argument. Granted, Republicans won back the House a year after that book was published. But some long-term demographic trends are not favorable to

Republicans. The GOP must continue to make the argument to African Americans that their natural home is the party of Abraham Lincoln, not the party of Southern Democrats such as George Wallace and Orval Faubus. But to do so, they'll have to adjust their brand, and that will not be easy.

Meanwhile, Republicans must seize opportunities to capture a sizable share of Latino voters, especially this election cycle. Sixty percent of the country's 31 million Latino adults are Catholic, and many of the rest are affiliated with Protestant denominations. As of 2008, Latinos made up 32 percent of all Catholics in America.[11] The Catholic Church, as you may have heard, is not happy with President Obama. The Obamacare requirement that Catholic institutions other than the church must provide contraceptive coverage is considered by many to be an attack on the faith's core beliefs. There are other reasons why Latinos should be a natural GOP constituency. Latinos often come from strong families that value faith and hard work. They or their parents left their homelands, often with limited language skills, to come to America to build a better life by the sweat of their brow. These are not people who want a handout from the federal government. The Democrats believe that Latinos are just one more group that they can pencil into their coalition, but Republicans are closing the gap. In 2006, Latino voters supported Democrats over Republicans in House races by a 69-30 margin. In 2008, they voted for Barack Obama over John McCain, 67-31. But in 2010, the margin was 60-38.[12]

However, the GOP may be letting this opportunity slip through its fingers. President George W. Bush had it right when he tried to introduce a compassionate approach to immigration that strengthened border security while offering a path to citizenship for undocumented aliens who already live here. Unfortunately, those efforts met with stiff resistance in his own party. Republicans also oppose other legislation, such as the DREAM Act providing citizenship to certain immigrants such as veterans, that could help the party make inroads with Latinos. Meanwhile, some of the rhetoric from the right is not endearing Republicans to the country's largest minority group. Republicans are right to be concerned about our country's terrible immigration efforts and porous borders, but the way they are making the argument is hurting the brand.

Still, I would choose Republicans' branding problems over Democrats' branding problems in a heartbeat. Let's go back to Trout and Ries. Their sixth law is "The Law of Exclusivity," which states, "When a competitor owns a word or position in the prospect's mind, it is futile to attempt to own the same word."[13] Earlier, I pointed out that Republicans can be described using eight words: less government, lower taxes, strong defense, traditional values. Those are some pretty good words, and many Democrats would like to have some of them or even all of them for their brand. Unfortunately for them, they can't get them because Reagan took them all for Republicans. He was first.

What eight words would Democrats use to describe themselves? I'm not sure they could do it in 800. President Carter was a Southern cultural conservative with a liberal's appreciation for government's role in the economy. Walter Mondale and Michael Dukakis were classic big government liberals. President Clinton was a New Democrat (a tacit admission that there was something wrong with the old kind) who believed in government but also had a heartlander's respect for traditional American self-reliance. What do Democrats stand for? I follow politics for a living, and I don't know.

The Democrats ought to be able to unite under the brand they once had: the party of the common man. If they did, they might own other words, like "equality," "justice" and "fairness." (I actually think Republican policies are more equal, just and fair, but this is a marketing book, not a policy book.) But they are too divided for that. While Republicans are united by Reagan's eight words, Democrats are a mishmash of powerful special interest groups that want something from the government: organized labor, rich lawyers, Hollywood liberals, environmentalists, abortion and homosexual rights supporters, etc. Certainly, various groups can coalesce to achieve an objective. The D-Day invasion of World War II was fought by American, British and Canadian troops along with French resistance fighters. But those different nationalities were successful because they shared an unquestioned common goal: the defeat of Hitler. The Democrats' coalition rarely is solidly united unless it has a common enemy – usually, Republicans who have held power in the White House for a long time. Occasionally that's enough to elect a Bill Clinton after 12 years of Reagan-Bush I and a Barack Obama after eight years of Bush II. But it's no way to win a branding war.

Moreover, the Democrats' branding signals are too mixed for the party to present a coherent message. They have wealthy donors just like Republicans do, and the party takes care of them quite effectively. Al Gore may have told Americans that he was for the people, not the powerful, as he did in the 2000 presidential campaign, but Americans knew that he was for the powerful as well – maybe not always the same powerful as the Republicans, but the powerful nonetheless. Those Hollywood liberals aren't exactly on food stamps. Moreover, Democrats have a mixed branding message crossing from the White House to statehouses across Arkansas. It's true that there are moderate Republicans in pockets across the country, particularly the Northeast, but there are almost no liberals. Democrats, on the other hand, are all over the board. There are still a number of conservative Democrats at the state and local levels in the South, though a lot of them are becoming former Democrats by defecting to the Republican Party. Those conservative Democrats who remain have a problem because they don't belong in that party. It's a problem for voters because they don't know where the party stands. And it's a problem for Democrats because it dilutes their brand.

The Democrats' biggest weakness has been obvious since before Reagan was elected president: They are the party of big government at a time when Americans say they don't want that. Americans are far more worried about big government (the entity associated with the Democratic brand) then they are with big business (the entity associated with the Republican brand). In a Gallup poll released in December 2011, far more Americans said big government (64 percent) is the biggest threat to the country than big business (26 percent). Another 8 percent cited big labor, also associated with the Democrats' brand. Almost half of all Democrats, in fact, cited big government as the bigger threat, while independents tracked alongside the average at 62-26-8.[14]

Democrats know that they are out of step with the people on the central issue of our time, which is the size and role of the federal government. And so, since Reagan, they have tried a "me, too" approach in which they have voted for big government policies while paying lip service to the idea that small government is actually better. They have said, "We are like the Republicans, just not so much."

I think you can figure out where I stand on that obvious inaccuracy, but, again, this book is not about policy. It's about branding, and when Democrats try to sell themselves as less-Republican Republicans, it hurts their brand. Democrats can never be the party of smaller government because Republicans already own that space. As Trout and Ries wrote In "The 22 Immutable Laws of Marketing," "You want to change something in a computer? Just type over or delete the existing material. You want to change something in a mind? Forget it. Once a mind is made up, it rarely, if ever, changes. The single most wasteful thing you can do in marketing is try to change a mind. ... In fact, what you often do is reinforce your competitor's position by making its concept more important."[15]

Once someone owns a word in the marketplace, it's almost impossible for a competitor to take it away. Instead, according to Trout, the competitor must find another word. In their book, Ries and Trout point to the marketing war between McDonald's and Burger King. Of the two, McDonald's has the stronger brand – in fact, one of the strongest brands in the world. Burger King's branding has been inconsistent. At one time, its "Have it your way" campaign offered an opposite and effective attribute that compared well to McDonald's' bag-it-and-sling-it approach. "Flame-broiling" also called to mind a burger being grilled to perfection as opposed to McDonald's' greasy fried process. But then Burger King adopted an unfruitful series of ad campaigns and became trapped in offering a "me too" approach. McDonald's long ago cornered the kids' market with Ronald McDonald and its playgrounds. So what did Burger King do? Built playgrounds and pushed its creepy Burger King mascot. According to Ries and Trout, what Burger King should have done is rip out its playgrounds and make itself the anti-kids' restaurant. If it had marketed itself as the place to go when it's time to grow up, 12-year-olds wouldn't be caught dead in McDonald's.[16] Instead, Wendy's became the fast food restaurant for grown-ups and captured the number two position in the market.

In the same way, no matter what Democrats do, they will never rebrand themselves as government-cutters. In fact, when Clinton said in his State of the Union address that, "The era of big government is over," he merely reminded voters of what Republicans had been saying all along.

So what should the party of more government do when Americans don't want more government? Democrats have two choices. One option is simply to stick to their guns and wait for the market to return to them, as it might eventually do. Politics is cyclical, and what's in fashion now (less government) can be replaced by its opposite later. In their book, "The 22 Immutable Laws of Branding," Ries and his daughter, Laura, wrote, "Markets may change, but brands shouldn't. Ever. They may be bent slightly or given a new slant, but their essential characteristics (once those characteristics are firmly planted in the mind) should never be changed. If the market swings another way, you have a choice. Follow the fad and destroy the brand. Or hang in there and hope the merry-go-round comes your way again. In our experience, hanging in there is your best approach."[17]

So what "slant" could that be? Instead of Democrats trying futilely to tell voters that they are also the party of less government, they could rebrand themselves as the party of a more effective government. In the 1980s, a group of moderate Democrats formed the Democratic Leadership Council, which had that very purpose, and it enjoyed one big success: Bill Clinton. Clinton was out of the New Democrat mold in that he supported an activist government, but not an excessive one, and he understood the political leanings of the American people. As president, he reduced the size of the bureaucracy by 373,000 workers,[18] reformed welfare (under great prodding by Republicans) and briefly balanced the budget (with a lot of help from Republicans). He enacted a series of what might be called small big-government policies that were popular with voters. He also offered himself as the opposite of Speaker of the House Newt Gingrich. Where Gingrich was undisciplined in his pronouncements, Clinton was measured. Where Gingrich was a policy wonk, Clinton was a people person. All Clinton had to do was wait for Gingrich to overstep his bounds. It's no wonder that, during the government shutdown of 1995, Republicans were blamed even though Clinton was equally at fault. Gingrich just seemed like the kind of guy who would do that, and besides, if the Democrats were the brand that liked government, why would they shut it down? It had to be the fault of the brand that hated government.

Had Obama followed in those footsteps, he would have been unbeatable in 2012. He already owned a great brand and a historic sentence: "He was the first black president." But today is the history we are living right now, and we know that when he entered office in a bad

An independent brand?

A word about independents. As I write this, Congress deservedly has some of its lowest approval ratings in history. Only about one in 10 Americans believes it is doing a good job, and I have to wonder who that one person is and how on earth he or she came to that conclusion. President Obama, a Democrat, has been well under 50 percent for many months. His predecessor, George W. Bush, a Republican, didn't exactly leave with sky-high approval ratings.

Given those realities, it might seem that this would be the year that someone outside of the two parties could have contended for the presidency. But for those who hope for that to happen – I'm sorry, but those hopes are likely to be dashed. Al Ries and his daughter, Laura, point out in their book "The 22 Immutable Laws of Branding," that two brands tend to dominate a category. In the business world, it's usually the leader and the alternative, and they do not switch places that often. Coke and Pepsi.

Walmart and Target. Home Depot and Lowe's.[19] In politics, it's going to be Democrats and Republicans.

Plus, remember the shopping cart paths that remained consistent regardless of store managers' efforts to change them? Americans long ago grew accustomed to shopping for candidates along a familiar path: turn right for the Republicans, turn left for the Democrats.

It's not likely that a third party will carve out a niche. What could happen would be something like the Ross Perot dynamic, where a single, charismatic figure with a lot of personal wealth bursts onto the scene temporarily. That candidate might make a difference in policy, as Perot did in increasing awareness of the need for a balanced budget. But he or she won't create a new brand. The two leading brands – Republicans as the party of less government; Democrats as the party of an activist government – are simply too entrenched.

economy, he took a typical liberal's approach to the problem and threw money at it. He enacted a massive short-term stimulus package paid for by tomorrow's taxpayers. Then, while the economy was still reeling, he pivoted to health care reform, greatly increasing the role of the government in a part of the economy in which it already had too big a role.

Obama's brand is set in stone: He's another big government liberal. Predictably, voters revolted in 2010 by replacing the House Democrats with Republicans and Speaker Nancy Pelosi with Speaker John Boehner.

It's possible that Democrats could expand their base, as Reagan did effectively in appealing to Reagan Democrats during the 1980s. But so often, Democrats have had limited success at that because their base gets so offended whenever the party supports policies that appeal to middle Americans. Obama is a good example. He has presided over some of the most extensive expansions of government in the country's history. He has tried to socialize part of the country's health care system. And STILL he has problems with members of his party's left, who think he should go much farther. In his book "BrandSimple," marketing guru Allan Adamson wrote, "The first rule when seeking to broaden the appeal of a niche brand is that you must identify a way to hold down both bases or risk losing everybody." In that respect, Bill Clinton, the master triangulator, may not have been a transformative leader, but he was a much more effective politician than Obama.

Some Democrats, of course, don't want the party to remain on its current path, and they don't want the party to reinvent itself. They really do want less government. For them, there is a simple solution: Become Republicans.

- 9 -

The Obama Brand

I'm going to spend the next two chapters doing something I wouldn't normally do: write mostly positive things about Barack Obama.

I couldn't be more opposed to his policies or the way he has governed this country. He came into office and threw money at the economy, burdening our children with trillions of dollars in additional debt. He has failed to address the soaring costs of Medicare and Social Security, which will bankrupt future generations. Obamacare is one of the worst ideas a president ever signed into law. He has added to the regulations that were already burdening employers. He has apologized for his own country and bowed to foreign leaders again and again. He has attempted to divide our country by class.

But as I have stated earlier, this is a book about branding. And, sigh, Obama is really good at that.

After being elected in 2004, Obama was not your typical first-term U.S. senator from Illinois. Instead, he was already a brand: the next big thing in politics. His staff was receiving 300 speaking invitations a week. His precondition for giving a speech on behalf of a candidate was a list of the event attendees' email addresses, enabling him to build up a huge database for his political action committee, Hopefund. His book tour for his political biography, "The Audacity of Hope," was a pseudo-campaign operation layered with political appearances.[1] By November, his advisors were actively considering a run.[2] In December 2006, he spoke to California's enormous Saddleback Church and then reached out to adherents of that other American religion, the National Football League, by appearing in an introduction for Monday Night Football. On Jan. 16, 2007, he filed his presidential exploratory committee papers and announced on his website that he was running. On Feb. 10, he made his formal announcement before 15,000 freezing supporters at the Old State Capitol in Springfield, Illinois, where Abraham Lincoln gave his "House Divided" speech in his 1858 Senate campaign against Stephen Douglas.[3]

Hillary Clinton, meanwhile, had spent the past six years rebranding herself. A polarizing figure from the 1990s, she had tried to remake herself into a respected U.S. senator from New York, though everyone knew she was running for president. However, her polling found she had a weakness: the public believed she had a tendency toward insincerity. Partly as a result of that, the campaign decided on a two-part branding strategy. The first was that she would not change her stance on any policies so she couldn't be accused of flip-flopping in order to get elected. The second was to make her seem the inevitable nominee.[4,5]

That meant Obama had a huge advantage in the branding war that would decide the outcome. Remember how the Law of Exclusivity says only one competitor can own a word? It was a change election, and Obama owned change. He was an African American with a not very American name – Barack Hussein Obama – who was new to the political scene. His name itself, in fact, sent a powerful branding signal that he was different, and we all know that difference is the most important concept in marketing. Meanwhile, although Clinton was running to be the first woman president, she had been a national figure since 1992. Everyone knew she was the most powerful first lady in history. No way could she own "change." Moreover, while Obama could never lose his "change" brand, Clinton's "inevitable" brand could be punctured, and Obama stuck it with a big needle in April 2007 when he announced that he had raised $25 million in the first quarter, almost all for use in the primaries and from a broad base of donors. Clinton had raised more money, $36 million, but $10 million of that had come from her Senate campaign and $6 million could only be used in the general election. He beat her even worse in the next quarter: $31 million to $21 million.[6]

How was he doing it? Part of it had to do with the candidate himself. Obama was not just a candidate but also a canvas on which individuals could paint their own vision of America. For African Americans, he was the dream of a new, more just society. For whites, he offered a chance to atone for the sins of the past. To play that up, Obama's campaign made sure he wasn't just speaking at a podium to a cheering audience. They placed the audience behind him so that viewers on television and the internet saw a multiracial tableau raptly listening to his soaring rhetoric. As Keith Reinhard, chairman emeritus of DDB Worldwide, said during the election, "Barack Obama is three things you want in a brand: New, different, and attractive. That's as good as it gets."[7]

But all of this did not just happen. The Obama campaign was involved in a sophisticated branding operation in which no detail was too unimportant.

Take, for example, the Obama logo. On Dec. 21, 2006, the not-yet-announced campaign asked designer Sol Sender, who had never before done political work, to design a logo for Obama within two weeks, and to do something different than had been done before.[8]

Sender brought a marketer's perspective to the task. He and his team looked at campaign designs from the past and saw a surprising uniformity. Whether the candidate was Republican or Democrat, their "logos," if you could call them that, were basically a variation of the candidate's name and a lot of red, white and blue. Determined to try to tell the candidate's story, he and his team read Obama's two books and found themes of hope and change. They also zeroed in on Obama's assertion that America is one country, not separate red and blue states. They thought it might be possible to create a logo that could be used without the candidate's name, which had not been done in American politics. At the same time, they didn't want it to be too different because their candidate was so nontraditional that questions about his patriotism might arise. The team eventually focused on the "O" in Obama's name, believing that it could be used to represent unity. The top half of the "O" became a blue sky, while the O's white center became a rising sun resting above red and white stripes that led into the distant horizon.[9,10]

The campaign loved it and, after choosing that idea Jan. 8, quickly began incorporating it into its efforts. When Obama announced he was running for president, his logo was affixed to the platform, although the printer mistakenly had removed the white "sun" in the middle of the "O," creating what Sender later joked was a "dark star."[11] Soon, if Obama went anywhere, his logo went with him. It was seamlessly incorporated into his literature, website and social media. The "O" was more than just a logo. It accomplished for Obama what the "Think Different" campaign had done for Apple. By branding itself as the company that unleashed a character trait rather than simply sold computers, Apple became what consumers wanted it to be – in fact, wanted themselves to be. The Obama logo, which began showing up EVERYwhere, evoked that same kind of response. It didn't really have to refer to a candidate. The rising (or setting?) sun, the red white and blue – a person could look at that and make it whatever they wanted, and it wasn't easily spoofed. That was a huge advantage over bumper stickers that featured the name of an actual, flawed candidate that voters could associate with a policy decision or statement they didn't like. The campaign brought in a branding team to watch over the logo and hired its own designers in the summer of 2007 to adapt it to different groups – a more crayon-ish one for kids, for example. Before the campaign was over, supporters were uploading their own photo to be placed inside the "O" on Flickr and decorating cookies and cupcakes in its image. A website showed how to carve the logo into a pumpkin.[11,12]

Hillary Clinton's logo? Her first name, which, granted, was a little creative, above the same squiggly little American flag design her husband had used. Not exactly the change voters were seeking.[13]

Meanwhile, Obama's campaign was fine-tuning its internet and social media efforts, which would be decisive in building support and helping him raise all that money. The website, BarackObama.com, was managed by Chris Hughes, who four years earlier had co-founded Facebook and now was taking a leave of absence to elect his candidate. By about six weeks before the Iowa caucuses, Hughes and his team had created a seamless website with a focused message and a design consistent with its Facebook and YouTube pages. The campaign chose a Gotham font, a simple, geometric typeface designed in America for GQ Magazine.[14] Every event, including every speech by Obama and, later, his vice presidential running mate, Sen. Joe Biden, was put on streaming video, bypassing the traditional media.[15] The site was updated often and featured photos, ringtones, and widgets.

The campaign created mybarackobama.com, its own social network, where people could blog about issues, send policy recommendations to the campaign, organize events, and even raise money. When Community Connect, a group of niche demographic websites including blackplanet.com and faithbase.com, asked the campaigns to create profiles for their targeted communities, the Obama campaign reacted far more effectively than the others, quickly earning 450,000 "friends." Andrew Rasiej, founder of the Personal Democracy Forum, a website studying technology and politics, told Fast Company magazine that Obama's campaign was "strategic and smart." "They've made sure the message machine was providing the message where people were already assembled," he said. "They've turned themselves into a media organization."[16]

The effect wasn't just to get the word out; it was to draw people in, to make them feel a part of something special, even if the Obama campaign didn't always clearly explain what that something special was. Karen Scholl, creative director at the digital-advertising agency Resource Interactive, told Fast Company that Obama was an "OPEN brand": on-demand, personal, engaging, and networked. She said that with Obama, "not only do people feel they know who he is, they feel trusted to share their views. And they get constant feedback from the campaign and from each other."[17] John Quelch, senior associate dean at Harvard Business School and coauthor of "Greater Good: How Good Marketing Makes for Better Democracy," pointed out the difference between Obama's people-centered communication skills and Clinton's policy wonkishness. People go to Starbucks, he said, "for the experience, not for the specifications of the coffee. Obama, through his inclusive website and, yes, his lofty rhetoric, reinforces the notion that everyone is included and that this movement is actually a conversation to which everyone is invited."[18]

Meanwhile, the Obama campaign was involved in a deft branding maneuver. The qualities that made him Brand Change also made him unprepared to be president. He was merely a state senator when he had made his famous speech before the Democratic National Convention in 2004, and all he had added to his resume since were a little more than two years of undistinguished service in the U.S. Senate (along with its most liberal voting record). He had to seem new, which he was, and also qualified, which he wasn't, so the campaign played to his strengths while trying to make people forget about his weaknesses. Speaking to students at the University of Oklahoma's Walker Arts Center on May 12, 2009, Scott Thomas, who managed the new media team for Obama for

America, said the campaign tried to present Obama as a hopeful, unifying figure of historical importance without making him seem aloof. In fact, Thomas said the campaign tried to project an image that Obama already was president. Since he wasn't prepared, at least his campaign would be. "The final mission was to establish a consistency and balance to exemplify stability and experience," he told students. "We knew that Barack was going to have this kind of Achilles' heel. He was a junior senator from Illinois, and it was important to us to make sure that we looked as professional as possible within the campaign on all levels, and that meant that using the same typeface and using the same hues of blue, and making sure that that was done iteratively over and over and over again, we would actually be able to in some way make this guy seem really experienced and organized, and I think that was really accomplished."[19]

In an interview with Newsweek magazine, graphic designer Michael Bierut expressed amazement at the campaign's ability to maintain such consistency throughout the long campaign.

"If you look at one of his rallies, every single non-handmade sign is in that font. Every single one of them. And they're all perfectly spaced and perfectly arranged. Trust me. I've done graphics for events, and I know what it takes to have rally after rally without someone saying, 'Oh, we ran out of signs. Let's do a batch in Arial.' It just doesn't seem to happen. There's an absolute level of control that I have trouble achieving with my corporate clients. ...

"I have sophisticated clients who pay me and other people well to try to keep them on the straight and narrow, and they have trouble getting everything set in the same typeface. And he seems to be able to do it in Cleveland and Cincinnati and Houston and San Antonio. Every time you look, all those signs are perfect. Graphic designers like me don't understand how it's happening. It's unprecedented and inconceivable to us. The people in the know are flabbergasted."[20]

While Obama had far and away the best campaign, he was not the best campaigner. During much of 2007, that title belonged to Clinton. She whipped him in a series of debates because she simply knew more about the issues. She also won some temporary battles in the branding war. Brand Inevitable started to stick. She raised more money in the third quarter and was leading Obama 53-20 in an ABC News/

Washington Post poll. Meanwhile, she had some success making herself a change candidate, though one that was different from Obama because she also had experience as a national leader. In September, the campaign adopted the slogan, "The Change We Need." In Concord, New Hampshire, Clinton campaigned with her husband on a stage set with banners displaying that message along with "Change + Experience." For a time, it was working. That same ABC News/Washington Post poll that found her leading 53-20 found voters seeking "new direction and new ideas" favoring Clinton 45-31.[21]

Clinton was running a mistake-free campaign until a debate Oct. 30 in which all the Democratic candidates were asked about then-New York Governor Eliot Spitzer's plan to allow illegal immigrants to be eligible for driver's licenses. Clinton defended Spitzer, saying he was reacting to the federal government's failure to create an effective immigration policy, but she did not express support for the policy itself. Connecticut Sen. Chris Dodd, whose candidacy was gong nowhere, pounced, accusing her of supporting the idea. The other candidates joined in the attack while she defended her remarks. Former South Carolina Sen. John Edwards and Obama accused her of trying to have it both ways. For several days, this minor event amidst a series of forgettable debates became the story. The reason it was sticking? Because the Hillary brand came with the baggage that saw her as calculating, triangulating and untruthful.[22]

As the Iowa caucus neared, Obama began pulling away. Buoyed by a dramatic increase in caucus-goers, he won easily on election night. Clinton not only lost to Obama but also to Edwards as well. In the midst of a change election, Obama, the ultimate nontraditional candidate, was making a victory speech amongst a sea of enthusiastic faces of all ages and races. Meanwhile, Clinton made her concession speech alongside relics from the past – her husband, former Secretary of State Madeleine Albright, and Gen. Wesley Clark.[23]

Clinton's Brand Inevitable was gone. Obama had reclaimed Brand Change. All she had left to sell was her tainted Brand Experience, and Obama's internal polls showed that New Hampshirites valued "change" over "experience" by a two-to-one margin.[24] Her money was drying up. African Americans, who had loyally stuck with her while they watched to see if Obama took hold, defected en masse.

But then something sort of amazing happened in New Hampshire: Clinton's brand changed there. It started with a debate January 5. Obama was riding high, and Edwards was still treating Clinton like a frontrunner. During the course of the debate, it became obvious that the two were teaming up on her – two men versus one woman. Then a questioner asked her what she would say to voters who believed Obama was more likable than she. "Well, that hurts my feelings," she said, mostly but not completely with mock hurt as the audience laughed and the questioner apologized profusely. "But I'll try to go on. He's very likable. I agree with that. I don't think I'm that bad." Obama looked up and said with only a hint of a smile, "You're likable enough, Hillary."[25]

Then, the day before the primary, Clinton was appearing in the morning's first campaign event, a discussion with independent voters at a coffeehouse in Portsmouth. Beforehand, her campaign manager had broached the idea of her gracefully quitting the race. No doubt Clinton was tired and discouraged as she saw her dream of becoming the country's first woman president slipping away. She was asked about the personal challenges of running for president. "It's not easy, and I couldn't do it if I didn't passionately believe it was the right thing to do," she responded. "You know, I have so many opportunities from this country. I just don't want to see us fall backward." And at that moment, tears came to Hillary Clinton's eyes, and her voice choked. "You know, this is very personal for me," she softly continued. "It's not just political. It's not just public. I see what's happening. And we have to reverse it."[26]

She had violated the cardinal rule of women in power: Thou shalt not cry in public. But Clinton was different. Part of her brand, and not a good part, was being an ice woman. The country had seen her stand coolly by her husband as he humiliated her with his indiscretions. They had seen her absorb harsh attacks and dish out some as well, all seemingly to further her nearly boundless ambition. The incident didn't make her look weak. It made her look human. Besides, the country had come a long way since Edmund Muskie had been forced from the 1972 race because of his real or apparent tears. Voters had watched both Bush presidents and Clinton's husband tear up while they were in office. After seeing that, and after watching those two men gang up on her in the debate, New Hampshire's undecided women broke her way. She won the state's primary, and it was a whole new race. In her victory speech, she sounded nothing like the cool policy wonk of the past. "Over the last week, I listened to you, and in the process, I found my own voice," she told a cheering crowd.[27]

In the race to reach 2,025 delegates, Clinton's win had evened the score at one state apiece. But in the branding wars, she was still losing. Brand Inevitable was gone. Obama still had Brand Change. Meanwhile, frustrated that the African American vote was slipping away from his wife's candidacy, Bill Clinton inserted himself into the campaign and inserted his foot into his mouth. In New Hampshire, Hillary had made a comment suggesting that Dr. Martin Luther King's dream had begun to become true because President Johnson had signed the Civil Rights Act into law. The comment was meant to stress the importance of the presidency, but it seemed to lessen King's accomplishments. Then Bill had called Obama's campaign a "fairy tale." Those comments were coming under scrutiny as being racially insensitive, and Bill didn't like it. In the midst of all that, he insisted on his wife competing in South Carolina, a state with a very large African American vote in the Democratic Party that some in the campaign would have preferred they skipped. There he became a media magnet, practically blowing his top at one campaign event. None of it helped the cause. Obama scored an impressive win, 55-27, that forced the third place-finishing Edwards from the race and made it a two-person contest. But Bill wasn't done. He dismissed the victory by saying that Jesse Jackson had won the state in 1984 and 1988. Some took it as a racially coded attack. As far as the delegate count, it was just another state Hillary had expected to lose anyway, but the effect on the branding war was far more devastating: Her husband had reminded the public of another aspect of Hillary's brand: that she was one half of a very complicated and often embarrassing marriage.[28]

The race continued. While voters were split evenly between the two candidates, Obama was opening up a cavernous fundraising lead thanks in large part to his far superior online operation. On Super Tuesday February 5, Clinton won four of the five largest states, but Obama won the smaller caucuses handily, earning more delegates that day than she did. Then Obama went on a roll, winning 11 straight contests. He still owned Brand Change, but now he was making a play for Brand Inevitable. Holding on to Brand Experience for dear life, her campaign released an ad depicting a 3 a.m. phone call in the Oval Office where she answered the phone. The implication was that she and not Obama was prepared for an international crisis.[29] The message may have helped, as she won Ohio and Texas.

And then Jeremiah Wright came along.

Obama had called Wright, the recently retired pastor of Obama's Trinity United Church of Christ in Chicago, his mentor. He had attended Wright's church for 17 years. Wright had officiated at Obama's wedding and baptized his daughters. Obama's 2006 autobiography, "The Audacity of Hope," drew its name from one of Wright's sermons. Wright was a member of Obama's African American Religious Leadership Committee that was advising the campaign.

Then on March 13, 2008, ABC News showed viewers footage of Wright preaching anti-American sermons, including one on the Sunday after September 11 when he blamed the United States for the attacks and another sermon in which he said, "God bless America? No, no, no! Not 'God bless America!' God damn America!"

It was at odds with Obama's racially neutral brand that had made him a black man with whom white Americans could feel comfortable. At first, Obama defended Wright, saying he was "like an old uncle who says things I don't always agree with,"[30] but it soon became obvious that the controversy would not go away. Trying to control the damage, Obama gave a speech on March 18 titled "A More Perfect Union" at Philadelphia's National Constitution Center flanked by four American flags in which he outlined America's racial history, repudiated Wright's remarks while defending him as a pastor, and even contrasted the sacrifices his own white grandmother had made for him with her own occasionally insensitive remarks.[31]

Wright would not go away. Offended by Obama's speech, he was unapologetic in an appearance on PBS and confrontational during an April 28 appearance at the National Press Club, where he praised Nation of Islam leader Louis Farrakhan and declared it possible that the government had tried to inflict African Americans with the AIDS virus. Obama now had no choice: maintain his relationship with his pastor or save his brand, because white Americans were never going to elect a candidate they associated with those comments. He repudiated his pastor. But his campaign, and his brand, had been damaged.[32]

Meanwhile, the Obama brand was suffering two other damaging

blows, both of them self-inflicted. Obama's wife, Michelle, twice said in Wisconsin Feb. 18 that she was proud of her country "for the first time" as an adult because of what was happening with her husband's campaign.[33] Many voters' first impression of her was that she was angry and anti-American. Not a good brand. That was nothing compared to what happened in a San Francisco fundraiser April 11, when Obama said that Pennsylvanians and Midwesterners who have struggled economically in recent years "cling to guns or religion or antipathy toward people who aren't like them or anti-immigrant sentiment or anti-trade sentiment as a way to explain their frustrations."[34] Coming on the heels of the Rev. Wright fiasco, Obama's "cling" comments threatened to brand him not only as a radical but as anti-Christian and anti-gun as well. Clinton pounced, calling the remarks "elitist and out of touch" and repeating again and again, "Americans need a president that will stand up for them, not a president that looks down on them."[35] Obama tried to explain that he meant to say, "When you're bitter you turn to what you can count on,"[36] apparently believing that people "count on" anti-immigrant sentiments the way they count on God. But coming less than two weeks before the Pennsylvania primaries, the remarks couldn't have been more ill-timed. Not surprisingly, Clinton won Pennsylvania easily.

But by then Obama's lead simply was too big for Clinton to catch up. He won North Carolina and almost won Indiana. On June 3, his victory in Montana, of all places, and the support of the party's elite superdelegates put him over the required 2,025 delegates. Out of 36 million votes cast in the primaries and caucuses, he had received only 150,000 more votes than Clinton, but it was enough. In St. Paul, Minnesota, the Obamas celebrated before a raucous crowd.[37]

Now it was on to the general election to face John McCain, Brand War Hero but also Brand More of the Same, and not nearly as good a campaigner as Hillary Clinton.

- 10 -

A Branding Mismatch:
Obama vs. McCain

If anyone wasn't a typical politician, it was John McCain. The son of Admiral John McCain, commander of the United States Pacific Command during the Vietnam War, he had been shot down and captured while flying a fighter jet mission over North Vietnam in 1967, leading to five and a half years of captivity that could have ended sooner had he accepted an offer of early release. He had refused because he didn't want to be used as a propaganda tool by the North Vietnamese. He became a United States senator from Arizona and began a career that was marked by honor, integrity and an independent spirit that occasionally annoyed his own party. In 2000, he ran for president, countering George W. Bush's massive fundraising advantage with a media-friendly campaign aboard his cleverly branded bus, the Straight Talk Express. He lost. Over the next few years, his reputation as a political maverick intensified. He opposed the 2001 Bush tax cuts and in 2002 co-authored the McCain-Feingold bill, which led to the passage of a law that regulated campaign financing and required candidates to make the "I approved this message" statement now tagged onto the end of campaign ads. A lot of Republicans hated McCain-Feingold and weren't too happy with McCain. Rush Limbaugh didn't have much complimentary to say about him, ever.

His 2008 campaign for the Republican nomination didn't go well at first, but he survived the early months until the actual voting began. The Iowa caucuses were won by former Arkansas Gov. Mike Huckabee, a Baptist preacher who carved out an interesting brand as a cheerful and hip religious conservative even liberals could like. However, Huckabee had no money, and 2008 wasn't a values election. Former Massachusetts Gov. Mitt Romney's Brand Competence would have to wait four years to catch the eye of Republican primary voters, while Rudy Giuliani's Brand Hero of September 11 could not overcome his disastrous campaign strategy. When McCain won New Hampshire and South Carolina, he solidified his status as the frontrunner and ultimately clinched the nomination before Obama finished off Hillary Clinton.

But Brand Maverick Straight-Talking War Hero faced an uphill battle. The country had grown weary of the wars in Iraq and Afghanistan, which McCain supported wholeheartedly. Because his party base had supported him only grudgingly, he had been forced to move to the right during the nomination fight and would have to stay there during the general election. That meant he was flip-flopping on the Bush tax cuts, which, coming from a supposed maverick, sent a mixed branding signal to the public. This was a change election, but McCain was a 72-year-old white guy who admitted he didn't know how to use a computer. In an election where three out of four voters were saying they wanted a president to lead in a different direction than President Bush, seven in 10 were saying that McCain would take the country in the same direction as Bush.[1] Small wonder that Obama was slightly ahead in the polls as the campaign began, and he was far ahead in fundraising. In fact, Obama was raking in so much dough that he decided to become the first candidate to say no to millions of dollars in public funds despite promising in November 2007 not to do that. McCain, the nominee of the "party of the rich," did not have that luxury. Thanks to Obama's huge fundraising advantage, he was able to spend more than twice as much as McCain on television advertising: $310 million to $136 million.[2]

Remember what was said earlier about the branding of campaigns being as important as the branding of candidates? Obama's team had won the campaign branding war before it even started. But on a personal level, Obama had to play catchup. For all of McCain the candidate's faults, McCain the patriot's brand was unassailable. No amount of advertising, positive or negative, could touch the grainy, black and white 1967 footage of a physically broken McCain lying in a North Vietnamese hospital bed. Meanwhile, Americans had serious questions about Obama's patriotism. Naturally, they would be suspicious of anyone named Barack Hussein Obama, but episodes that merely would trouble Democratic primary voters, like the Rev. Wright controversy and the "cling" comment, would be disqualifying to many voters in a general election. Moreover, there were other snippets that were making their way around the internet, such as a photo of Obama standing with his hands at his side instead of having his hand over his heart during the playing of the national anthem. (Emails incorrectly said it was during the Pledge of Allegiance.) He made a point of not wearing a flag pin on his lapel because he said it would have been a false show of patriotism. That would have been a reasonable argument coming from John McCain, Brand War Hero, not Barack Obama, Brand We're Not Sure If He's Proud to be an American. Despite the Rev. Wright controversy, many Americans believed he was a Muslim.

There was no way Obama was going to be the more patriotic candidate. His campaign thought it could, on the other hand, make him the more presidential one. Shortly after winning the nomination, he left the campaign trail and embarked on a 10-day, eight-country tour that included Kuwait, Afghanistan and Iraq and continued to Europe, where he spoke before a throng of 200,000 in Berlin. It was an impressive trip even for those who did not like Obama, particularly when he coolly hit a three-point basketball shot in Kuwait without a warm-up to the cheers of hundreds of soldiers.[3]

Aware they were losing the election, McCain's advisers decided to use Obama's worldwide celebrity against him. They created an ad, "Celeb," that displayed Obama's picture with Brittney Spears and Paris Hilton and featured him speaking before huge crowds with a sound track of cult-like supporters chanting his name. "He's the biggest celebrity in the world, but is he ready to lead?" a female narrator asked. It worked. McCain's campaign had done what Hillary Clinton had not been able to do: find a way to rebrand Obama. In 30 seconds, the campaign introduced Americans to the idea that Obama was empty and selfish – just another celebrity – compared to McCain, who had remained in a Hanoi prison for his country. Obama's negatives began to rise. By August 1, the campaign was tied in the polls.[4]

The Democratic National Convention in Denver would reverse that. Michelle Obama, who entered the convention as Brand Female Black Panther, was transformed by her convention speech into Brand Loving Wife and Mother. For Obama's speech, the convention was moved out of the Pepsi Center and onto Invesco Field, home of the Denver Broncos, where he spoke before a throng of more than 100,000.

Once again, Obama threatened to run away with the campaign, and once again McCain's camp would have to react. In order to recapture his reputation as Brand Maverick and make a dent in Obama's Brand Change, McCain needed to make a splash with his vice presidential selection. He couldn't nominate another old white Republican man. For a while he strongly considered Sen. Joe Lieberman, Al Gore's running mate in 2000 who had been re-elected as an independent and had announced his support for McCain. But members of the Republican base would not support a pro-choice Democrat.

They would, however, support Alaska Governor Sarah Palin. Palin had risen to power by bucking the system, including her own party, which made her a perfect complement to the maverick McCain. While he was old and worn, she was young and attractive, even sexy, though she did little to encourage that aspect of her public persona. She also allowed McCain to at least get into the game in a change election. While Obama would be the nation's first black president, she could be the first female vice president. Meanwhile, she was a young mother to whom average Americans could relate.

Palin immediately rebranded the McCain campaign as young and vivacious at the same time it diluted Obama's change message. Her nomination and electric acceptance speech at the Republican National Convention energized the base and flipped white women from supporting Obama 50-42 to backing McCain 53-41.[5] For a time the Obama campaign and its allies in the national media did not know what to do with her. Then Tina Fey of "Saturday Night Live" went on the attack with her withering impression, while Palin's own shaky performance in a series of interviews with CBS news anchor Katie Couric left many Americans wondering if she was prepared to be president.

Despite the Palin hiccup, Obama would win the branding war decisively from that point forward. His campaign's narrative – that 2008 would be an election of hope and change embodied by a candidate unlike any Americans had elected before, was a perfect fit for the times. McCain's campaign, meanwhile, was less successful at developing a narrative even though one was readily available – the war hero fighting one last battle for the America he loved. After bouncing between slogans and story lines, the campaign finally settled on "Country First," which should have happened much earlier.

Meanwhile, the Obama campaign set a new standard for attracting eyeballs and donors on the internet. Campaign messages targeted different population segments – texts for young people, emails for older voters. The campaign effectively used microtargeting, a technique that will be covered in the next chapter where voters are segmented according to their buying and online habits and then reached accordingly. Another benefit of going on offense online was that the campaign didn't have to play as much defense. With numerous campaign-generated viral videos bouncing around the internet, surfers who Googled "Barack Obama" were greeted with positive links about him on the search engines' front pages rather than critical analyses or crazy rumors. As the campaign neared its end, the campaign sent daily messages to supporters, even creating a contest where donors could enter a lottery to attend the Election Night victory party.[6]

The Obama campaign was so successful online because it had what Andrew Rasej, founder of TechPresident.com, called a "culture of belief in the internet," starting with the candidate. McCain, meanwhile, had no such belief. His campaign tried to catch up to Obama by creating its own digital video products but lacked the online strategy and the candidate to make that content go viral. In July, BarackObama.com had twice as many hits as JohnMcCain.com, and by September, that margin had not changed.[7]

McCain's logo, with its Optima font and military star, was symbolic of his campaign's inability to compete with Obama's marketing strategy. Intended to emphasize his war record, it instead looked outdated – sort of like the candidate. It also wasn't the best message to send to a war-weary public growing increasingly disenchanted with America's involvements in Afghanistan and Iraq. It couldn't be adapted for anything beyond a bumper sticker or a yard sign. Moving McCain's name up and putting "Palin" beneath it when he announced his running mate was all that could be done.

Obama's branding prowess and internet presence served him well in an election cycle that was changing many of the established rules, including when voters solidified their support for candidates. Traditional wisdom was that voters didn't really pay attention until after Labor Day, but the internet and the 24-hour news cycle were turning that on its head. Voters who had access to a never-ending stream of information from Twitter, Facebook and other sources were making up their minds earlier than in the past, and that favored the candidate with a stronger brand and an immediate online presence that could reach them when it mattered.

But while Obama's online efforts remained a key part of the campaign, much of the most important work occurred offline using old-fashioned voter contact – in other words, the kind of one-on-one, word of mouth marketing that focuses on personal contacts and finding influencers. In "The Face to Face Book" by Ed Keller and Brad Fay, Jon Carson, the Obama campaign's field director, explained, "At the end of the day, voter contact happened because trained field organizers got their volunteers into a system that was getting doors knocked and phone calls made. ... To win these Republican states, you have to persuade a lot of people who had never voted for a Democrat before. A lot of that is peer pressure, frankly. And so we put a top premium on local volunteers talking to their neighbors."[8]

In order to make that happen, the Obama campaign went to an unlikely source of inspiration: George W. Bush's 2004 campaign, which practiced what Bush chief strategist Matthew Dowd described to Keller and Fay as "echo politics": getting supporters to talk to their friends and neighbors, write letters and call talk radio shows about Bush policies such as the war in Iraq. The idea was to create credibility and make people receptive to a campaign message they had already heard from their like-minded friends and neighbors.

Dowd had created the strategy after realizing that the number of true independent swing voters had fallen to less than seven percent of the electorate by 2002. (Remember, we're all branded.) That meant that the key to victory lay not in trying to convince those people as to the rightness of the cause but rather in awakening passive Republican voters, and the best way to do that wasn't simply through a barrage of television commercials but through word of mouth and by mobilizing what the campaign called "navigators," or people of influence. The campaign selected about 2 million navigators from an email list of seven million volunteer Bush supporters by using sophisticated data mining techniques that we'll discuss in more detail later. Those navigators were sent a flow of campaign emails with talking points and tips on how to get past talk radio screeners. They proved decisive in the final days, especially in the battleground state of Ohio. While Kerry's campaign was relying on traditional last minute efforts such as bringing in out of state volunteers, the navigators were influencing their friends and neighbors. "The information flow has become a flood, a torrent of messages coming at a confused, cynical public from all angles," Dowd told the authors. "People are turning to one another once again. As they did a century ago, today's opinion leaders work on the grassroots level rather than from the high perches of media, politics, or business. The twenty-first century opinion leaders are average Americans who know lots of other average Americans, trusted souls with large social networks. These navigators are influencing public opinion one casual conversation at a time."[9] They proved to be critical. Bush won a close vote in Ohio and, because of that, won the election.

So Obama owned a change brand in a change election. He had the best online presence in the history of American politics. He had a strong, motivated field organization. And he was facing a candidate who didn't appreciate how elections were won.

Then the already shaky economy began to collapse. What was left of the housing bubble burst. Some of the biggest names in American finance – Lehman Brothers, AIG, Fannie Mae, Freddie Mac – were crumbling at the same time that McCain's fellow Republican, George W. Bush, happened to be in the White House.

McCain fumbled his response. First he said the economy's "fundamentals" were strong. Then he called the situation "a total crisis."[10] Then he said he would fire the chairman of the Securities and Exchange Commission if he were president – a power the president does not have. Then he decided to suspend the campaign, postpone a debate with Obama, and return to Washington to see what he could do about the situation. In the process, he cancelled an appearance with David Letterman, earning days of scorn from the TV host. Once he arrived in Washington, he accomplished nothing. Then McCain said the debate was back on. When it occurred, most agreed that Obama won.

The whole episode badly damaged McCain's brand. A month before the election, McCain became Brand Erratic and, for the first time in the campaign, Brand Maybe Too Old.

By the time Election Day arrived, the outcome was not in doubt. Even McCain, the man who doggedly had spent five-and-a-half years in prison, gave up. Days before the vote, he and his wife, Cindy, appeared on "Saturday Night Live" in a skit where the joke was that they were trying to raise campaign cash through a Home Shopping Network-like scheme. Obama won 375 electoral votes to McCain's 163. He won 53 percent of the popular vote, collecting nearly 10 million more votes than McCain and earning the highest percentage of any Democrat since Lyndon Johnson.

Obama won the 18-29-year-old vote, 66 percent to 32 percent – by far the largest percentage won by a Democrat in recent history. That's not surprising given that he was so much closer to those voters in age than McCain. However, age was hardly the only factor. Obama's brand simply was a better fit for young people than McCain, and his campaign knew how to build that brand by using the power of the internet and word of mouth marketing. Besides, young people will vote for old people. In 1984, Ronald Reagan won almost 60 percent of the youth vote campaigning against the much younger Walter Mondale, and George H.W. Bush outpolled Democrat Mike Dukakis four years later. In recent elections, Rep. Ron Paul's army has largely been led by young libertarians.

The accolades rushed in. Before the election even occurred, the Association of National Advertisers voted Obama its Advertising Age Marketer of the Year. [11] In a column published the day after the election, Al Ries gushed in Advertising Age, "Nov. 4, 2008, will go down in history as the biggest day ever in the history of marketing. Take a relatively unknown man. Younger than all of his opponents. Black. With a bad-sounding name. Consider his first opponent: the best-known woman in America, connected to one of the most successful politicians in history. Then consider his second opponent: a well-known war hero with a long, distinguished record as a U.S. senator. It didn't matter. Barack Obama had a better marketing strategy than either of them. 'Change.'"[12]

Ries wrote that Obama's unchanging "change" message contrasted with Clinton and McCain, neither of whom could come up with a consistent message. Both were aware it was a change election and that Obama embodied that, so they had responded by arguing that they could enact change better than he could. Which was a fatal mistake.

"'Better' never works in marketing," Ries declared. "The only thing that works in marketing is 'different.' When you're different, you can pre-empt the concept in consumers' minds so your competitors can never take it away from you."[13]

The nation's professional marketers were so impressed with Obama's campaign that they began to copy it. Pepsi began a "Choose Change" campaign. Ikea adopted an "Embrace Change '09" campaign. And Southwest Airlines began selling "Yes You Can" tickets.[14]

Of course, after the election is when Obama started to govern, and the change we got was bigger government and Obamacare. He campaigned as a newer version of Reagan, and when he got into office, he pulled off the mask and underneath was Jimmy Carter.

Maybe that's another book.

- 11 -

Brand Conservative Woman

My reaction was the same as everyone else's: Sarah who?

When John McCain announced in August 2008 that he'd selected Sarah Palin as his vice presidential running mate, the 44-year-old was probably best known for being the subject of a bumper sticker that read, "Alaska: Coldest State, Hottest Governor." Within a few days, she was the hottest name in politics. Her tough, funny speech at the Republican National Convention made her a household name and a hero to many. The moment when she stood beside McCain and waved to the crowd while her hunky husband, Todd, stood behind her holding their baby was a transformative one in American political history. For a time, she eclipsed her running mate. Americans had long grown accustomed to the idea that a man Palin's age could run for president despite having children at home; in recent years, Carter, Clinton and George W. Bush had done so. But they had never seen a young mother in a position to someday lead the free world. And they probably didn't expect the first to be a Republican.

Palin's nomination marked a sea change that already was occurring in American politics and then accelerated because of her. A total of 269 women, including 174 Democrats and 95 Republicans, have served in the Congress throughout American history, many of them in recent years. The total number of women in Congress rose from 3 percent in 1979 to 16.8 percent in 2009. According to the Center for American Women and Politics, at last count there were 90 currently serving – 73 in the House and 17 in the Senate. Most are Democrats, but Republican women are making gains. Five of the 17 senators are Republicans, the same number as following the 2008 elections, but the number of female Republican House members has increased from 17 to 24.[1]

Maybe the most important gains have occurred in state governments, particularly in governor's mansions. Four of the nation's six female governors are Republicans: Jan Brewer of Arizona, Susana Martinez of New Mexico, Mary Fallin of Oklahoma, and Nikki Haley of South Carolina. Seven of the nation's 11 lieutenant governors are Republicans.[2] Republican women gained more than 100 seats in state legislatures in 2010.[3]

How big a year was 2010 for Republican women? Every incumbent Republican woman who was running for a federal or statewide office was re-elected. Two of the new Republican women governors, Martinez and Fallin, defeated Democratic women. Seventeen Republican women ran for the Senate and 128 for the House.[4] Sixty of the 106 women challenging House incumbents were Republicans.[5] Thanks in part to these strong women candidates, House Republicans won the women's vote for the first time since exit polling started being studied in 1982. Republicans won by 12 points, 56-44, among women over 60.[6]

We shouldn't treat the 2010 election as a slam dunk. Before 2010, the numbers of Republicans had held relatively steady for about a decade. While a record number of Republican women filed and ran in the primaries that year, their success rate was much lower than the Democratic women who ran. According to Debbie Walsh with the Center for American Women and Politics, Democratic women won 46 percent of their primaries, while Republican women won 28 percent of theirs. Because so many Republican men also won, by the time all the votes were counted, Republican women remained about the same percentage of the caucus as they were before.[7]

But the arc of history is bending. Republican women didn't hit double digits in the House of Representatives until the 1980 election, when Reagan beat Carter. There were never more than two Republican women in the Senate until after the 1994 elections.

Who are these new Republican leaders who were elected in 2010? Most are conservative on social issues, but they are more likely to talk about cutting taxes, repealing Obamacare or reducing the national debt. Some are straight out of the Palin model. Rep. Kristi Noem of

South Dakota, who was elected in 2010, is a 40-ish mother of three. Rep. Jaime Herrera Beutler from Washington is 33 and the first person of Hispanic descent to represent the state of Washington. Rep. Sandy Adams of Florida earlier in life served as a deputy sheriff. Rep. Diane Black of Tennessee, Rep. Ann Marie Buerkle of New York, and Rep. Renee Ellmers of North Carolina are all nurses, and Buerkle is also a lawyer. Rep. Nan Hayworth of New York is an ophthalmologist. Rep. Vicky Hartzler of Missouri and her husband own three farm equipment stores. Sen. Kelly Ayotte of New Hampshire, previously the state's attorney general, is 44 and a wife with two children living at home. Rep. Martha Roby of Alabama, also a young mother, is an attorney.

So why the surge of women, particularly conservative women, in politics? Part of it starts with the changing role of women in society. Of course, women have gained power as they have entered the workplace. Indeed, according to the Center for Women's Business Research, about 40 percent of privately held firms are at least 50 percent owned by a woman.[8] Moreover, women will gain power in the coming years because they are better educated than their male counterparts. About 57 percent of students enrolled in American colleges from at least 2000 to early 2010 were women.[9] Nationwide, American women have more than 1.2 million more college degrees than American men. In 2010, nearly six out of 10 adults holding advanced degrees between the ages of 25 and 29 were women. Women also are proving adept at using the tools of the 21st century. A study done by the research firm Harris Interactive found that 68 percent of women use social media to stay in touch with loved ones and co-workers, compared to 54 percent of men.[10] Women also have enormous power as consumers. Middle-aged women make 80 percent of all health care decisions in America,[11] which may explain why, in the wake of Obamacare, three female Republican nurses and an ophthalmologist were elected to Congress. Finally, women vote. According to the Center for American Women in Politics, women have outvoted men in every presidential election since 1964. In 2008, according to self-reported numbers, women outvoted men 70.4 million to 60.7 million.[12]

In the past, women in politics tended to be liberal Democrats, partly for cultural and partly for political reasons. Culturally, conservative women had a more traditional view of their role in society and in the home, so they were less likely than feminists to feel comfortable stepping into what had always been a man's role. Politically, they may have bought into the stereotype that a "woman's issue" always either involved bigger government – government-funded child care, for example – or abortion from the pro-choice perspective. Until recently, the media almost always looked for a liberal Democrat to speak on those issues, ignoring the historical fact that two of the most important leaders in the women's suffrage movement, Susan B. Anthony and Elizabeth Cady Stanton, were pro-life.

Even today, many conservative women remain reluctant to run. They fear harming their families and subjecting themselves to the spotlight that comes with campaigning for office. Rep. Cathy McMorris Rodgers from Washington, who was elected in 2004, is also a young mother – in fact, she is the only member of Congress who has given birth to two children while serving. She has tried for years to get more Republican women to run for office, often without success. Most women are too busy, and politics simply hasn't been a major priority. She said women tend to wait to be asked, and even then it takes them two years to decide to do it. "It's relatively new for there to be younger women serving in Congress that are married with kids and a family – you know, moms and such," she said. "I think I was the fifth woman ever to give birth while serving in Congress."[13]

But, according to Rodgers, that may be changing because conservative women no longer can ignore how decisions made in Washington affect their families. Now that they have seen others run for office, more are taking the plunge.

There is one other reason why more Republican women are running for office and winning: They have a great brand.

Voters, as you may have noticed, are disgusted with politics as usual, and the usual politicians are men. Just like Obama was able to do in the presidential race, a female politician sends a powerful branding signal that she is different than what we have seen before. After decades of dirty politics and tawdry sex scandals involving male politicians – from Gary Hart to Bill Clinton to the toe-tapping senator from Idaho, Larry Craig – women are looking good in comparison. Most folks know that women in their forties and fifties, especially those with children, aren't inclined to have affairs and certainly don't have time for them.

And compared to Democratic women, some of whom wear their feminism like a facial tattoo, Republican women seem approachable and trustworthy. Voters know these moms share their values. They also appreciate that they have run their homes, juggled family responsibilities, managed family budgets, and put up with their husbands. Who better to elect to Congress?

The polling firm American Viewpoint confirmed these observations by conducting three surveys of non-liberal women from January 2009 to April 2010 for the Republican National Committee. In its last survey, it also polled 300 men. It also conducted five focus groups from January 2009 to March 2010 – mostly of women but also of a few men. In head to head comparisons between a generic Republican woman versus a generic Democratic man or woman among ticket-splitting female voters, the Republican woman came out far ahead in many important areas. The Republican woman had a 21 point lead when asked about honesty and trustworthiness, a 16 point lead when asked if the candidate would not be controlled by special interests, and a 10 point lead when asked who would best work across party lines to accomplish things. Republican women got high marks for being better communicators, independent, emotionally connected and family-oriented. Significantly, the generic Republican woman had a 30 point lead in one of the most important policy areas – fiscal responsibility. Going into 2010, the group found that the overall Republican brand had a problem with women, who were unhappy with former President Bush and who saw the party as being old, rigid and in danger of being obstructionist. But female candidates had an advantage that counteracted some of the weaknesses in the Republican brand. The women voters saw them as being good listeners, fiscally responsible, honest and better able to understand the voters' daily lives.[14]

Rep. Rodgers sees that dynamic occurring as she works to recruit and elect women Republicans. "I think, yes, that there is just an inclination to view a woman as being trustworthy and honest," she said in an interview. "I guess one of the things that I see is that, for a number of men, running for Congress is another rung in the ladder, and a lot of men are driven by success and climbing that ladder of success. And for a number of women, I think our motivation is different in that for a lot of women who get involved in politics, it is they are compelled to get involved because of the cause – especially when that cause involves their families and children."[15]

Suzanne Terrell sees it much the same way. Terrell was elected Louisiana elections commissioner in 1999, ran unsuccessfully for Senate in 2002 against Democrat Mary Landrieu, and then helped create two groups: Project GoPink, an organization that encourages Republican women to run for office, and ShePAC, a political action committee to elect Republican women. According to Terrell, "I've had this discussion with many, many, many people. ... Are women more honest? Are women less likely to have an affair? And I tend to say I think it's the nature."[16]

Terrell sees a similar advantage for Republican women over their Democratic counterparts, many of whom are stuck in the 1960s and make a point of not being judged by their looks. Like Palin and Rep. Michelle Bachmann, most of the Republican women don't see an inconsistency with serving their districts while also looking professional and attractive. They are strong, not strident. "If that's part of the brand that people are saying, 'Well, Republican women are better looking, so I'm going to vote for them,' have at it," Terrell said. "If you want to vote for me because you like my eyes, I'll take your vote. I don't think the Democratic women look at it that way. If somebody says to a Democratic woman or to a liberal or a, quote, feminist, 'I'm voting for you, honey, because I think you have great eyes,' they'd probably slug them. If somebody said to me, 'I'm voting for you, honey, because you've got great eyes,' I'd say, 'Thank you very much, and I hope I can do a great job for you when I'm in office.'"[17]

That doesn't mean Terrell wants women judged on their sex appeal. In fact, her group, ShePAC, is ready to fight against sexist treatments of women candidates, particularly when it involves liberal media hypocrisy. When the "entertainer" Bill Maher crudely attacked Sarah Palin and other conservative women and then made a million dollar donation to Obama's SuperPAC, the media stood silent. ShePAC did not. It produced a video highlighting the hypocrisy and saw its donations increase. ShePAC is supporting women candidates like Mia Love, the daughter of Haitian-American immigrants who is running for a House seat in Utah.[18] It's made a major commitment this year to five Senate candidates: Deb Fischer from Nebraska; Sarah Steelman from Missouri; Linda Lingle from Hawaii; Linda McMahon from Connecticut;

and Heather Wilson from New Mexico. If elected, they would break the Democrats' stranglehold on the Senate.

A discussion about the Republican woman brand wouldn't be complete without considering the challenges that come with it. There is the aforementioned problem with being seen as sex objects. You won't see any of these conservative women – and some of them are quite attractive – dressing immodestly. After Palin was nominated, males across the country began googling "Sarah Palin" and "hot" looking for sexy pictures. The most anyone could find was a photo of her in a pair of cute running shorts that had been taken for Runner's World that was then reprinted on the cover of Newsweek. There was also a fuzzy 40-second clip of Palin walking across the stage in a bathing suit in the 1984 Miss Alaska Pageant.

Also, as did Palin, Republican moms must answer questions Republican dads never get asked – namely, why aren't you home with the kids? Those questions come from all sides, including fellow Republicans. During her race, Martha Robey was asked that question by the older woman who challenged her in the GOP primary.

"There is a reason that when women run for office when they have young children, they're reluctant to put their kids' pictures all over the place," said Debbie Walsh with the Center for American Women in Politics. "For a man to have a brochure with the attractive wife, the lovely three kids and the golden retriever, it's fabulous. It's the old Mastercard line, right? It's priceless. It shows that you have an investment in the community and a stake in the future, that you're a family person, a family man just like they are or just like they wish they were. And it's really worth something. When women run, what happens is if they were to try to do that same kind of brochure ... that same kind of website, the first question that comes up is, 'Well, who's going to take care of your children if you get elected to office?' Nobody asks that of the men."[19]

Terrell has been fighting the fight for a long time and has the battle scars to prove it, and her experience is instructive for conservative women running for office. The only Republican woman ever elected to a statewide position in Louisiana, she hadn't intended to run for the U.S. Senate against Democrat Mary Landrieu in 2002 until the leading Republican candidate made a major gaffe and began dropping in the polls. Soon afterwards, she received a phone call from the Republican

Senatorial Committee about her running. Sen. Bill Frist committed to funding her $465,000 if she could make it into a runoff against Landrieu in Louisiana's open primary. That meant hanging tough with Landrieu while finishing in front of two male Republican contenders who, she decided, didn't want to lose to a girl. One of her distant cousins was the widow of Ted Kennedy, whom she had met once. That supposedly made her a Kennedy clone. "During the primary, mine was more, 'I'm the best candidate to take her on. Our goal here is to defeat Mary Landrieu,'" she said in an interview. "My two opponents' goal was to run me into the ground the best ways that they could."[20]

Terrell did finish second and made it into a runoff against Landrieu, which occurred a few weeks after the election. The only national race left after everything had been decided, it generated a huge amount of interest and publicity. They debated on "Meet the Press." The campaign became very negative – which, of course, resulted in the obligatory "catfight" comments. The state's male Republican governor, who originally had supported the big-mouthed congressman, made a comment about the two bitchy women running against each other. Terrell's favorability ratings, which had been high before the race, fell. "I get into the runoff with her, and now I have to soften my image, right? First I had been a bitch," she said. "Now, I'm too much of a bitch, so I've now got to become someone nice, because people vote for nice. People vote for someone they want to have in their own house, they want to have dinner with or coffee."

The process was difficult for Terrell not only as a candidate but as a mother. She had made a commitment that she would not put her family in financial jeopardy to further her political career, that she would not take out a second mortgage on her house or tap into her family's retirement or college funds. She also committed to having dinner with her family every night possible and attending her daughter's volleyball games – commitments she kept. Every candidate says that kind of thing, of course, but according to Terrell, "It doesn't ring as (equally) true, I think, when a man says it."

"Generally the woman is the nurturer of the household and generally the person that children turn to and the role model in my household because I have only daughters," she said. "So it was important for me to be out there. It wasn't something I thought about, 'Oh, do I need to be out there and prove I can do this for my kids?' No, but it was important that when I took on something that was hard in a professional sense, that they could see that I was strong and capable when I was doing it, that I met whatever the bar was, or the stereotype."

As the campaign wore on, Terrell discovered one of her most powerful speech lines was one she had used previously: "I live 13 doors away from where I grew up, and my mother lives 13 parishes away from where she grew up, and I don't want my children living 13 states away looking for a job. I want to be able to visit my grandchildren in the same city that I live in, or at least in the same state." It would have worked had she been a man, of course, but it had special relevance coming from a woman. She had to fight with her consultant about putting her children in a television ad. When she finally prevailed, the ad closed with her daughter saying something like, "If my mom can handle three daughters, she can handle anything they throw at her in Washington." People still talk to her about it.

However, it wasn't enough to win the election. She knew she was in trouble when, while speaking at a factory on the morning of the vote, someone asked, "Well, did you and the governor ever get yourselves straight?" Landrieu won. As Terrell was getting ready to walk out on stage that night, she turned to her family and announced that they were not going to cry. "That was because I didn't want to appear to be a bad loser," she said. "I didn't want to appear to be a weak woman."[21]

No one who has talked to her could think that.

- 12 -

The Branding of You, Part Two

After 35 years of counseling married couples, Dr. Neil Clark Warren, a clinical psychologist, decided that successful marriages usually involved two people who were compatible from the start, while those that ended in divorce involved incompatible people whose differences couldn't be resolved over time.[1] He learned that the old "Opposites attract" concept was only half true. The reality, as he would often say later, is that "Opposites do attract, and then they attack."[2] He decided to improve on the traditional way of finding a mate – trying to choose and then woo one person out of the multitude – by launching the online dating site eHarmony. After paying a fee and answering hundreds of questions about themselves that were created by relationship experts, customers were given a list of matches to choose from.

Well, that's how it used to work. In recent years, eHarmony is about math as much as it is psychology. In addition to the personal questions, the company also analyzes how a user behaves online – for example, how long it takes him or her to respond to an email that has information about a match. Experience has shown those behaviors say a lot about how a person will act in a relationship.[3]

The questions, the behavioral samples, and the mathematical algorithms that tie it all together are based on the same simple idea we discussed in chapter five: Although people are complex individuals, if you can find out their tendencies, you can place them into groups and predict how they will behave most of the time. You've seen that idea in action if you have ever taken a Keirsey Temperament Sorter, which describes people as one of four types, or a Myers Briggs Type Indicator test, which places them into one of 16 categories. For eHarmony, the practice must be working. The company claims that 542 people who use its service marry every day in the countries where it is available: the United States, Canada, Australia and the United Kingdom.[4] As of 2010, it was collecting $250 million a year in annual revenue.[5]

That's what political campaigns are doing these days, too – looking for compatible matches by combining the questions-based techniques of eHarmony and the predictive analytics described in chapter five. In other words, political campaigns aren't just branding themselves, as we learned earlier in this book. They are branding you.

Voters have long been divided according to income, gender, race and other factors. Suburban white people tend to vote Republican; African Americans tend to vote Democrat. Campaigns also can determine if a person is likely to vote for a certain candidate based on their voluntary memberships in politically active organizations. For example, people join labor unions because they support collective bargaining, so they are more likely to support Democrats. Members of the National Rifle Association support candidates who are strong on gun rights – usually Republicans but also some Democrats, particularly in the South. Meanwhile, campaigns have known that certain television and radio shows and print publications attract certain types of readers. For example, candidates wouldn't run an ad during Saturday morning cartoons, or buy a spot in Car and Driver magazine touting their support of higher gas taxes.

Now, through a practice known as microtargeting, campaigns can take this to another level. They can find out who people are, find out what they buy, put them into groups, and then target members of the group with a specific message knowing that most of its members probably vote alike. They do this by studying demographic information, online activities, and purchasing habits and then conducting a large phone survey. Virginia-based Target Point Consulting, in fact, will survey 10,000 of them.[6] Michael Meyers, the firm's president, told Fast Company in 2008 that it had defined 30 "major DNA strands within the electorate," including soccer moms and NASCAR dads, and then targeted those groups with individual messaging.[7]

During a campaign, those messages come in the form of phone calls, direct mail, a knock on the door, email – all tailored to a particular voter. Unlike broadcast television ads that are the same for every viewer, online political ads that appear on voters' screens match their interests and history.

Remember what Trout and Ries wrote In "The 22 Immutable Laws of Marketing" about how impossible it is to change a person's mind? Campaigns don't waste their time or their candidate's money trying to do that, so they look for voters in one of four camps: Republicans, Democrats, people who can be persuaded, and nonvoters. Campaigns don't mess with voters who are firmly in the other party's camp. In fact, they hope they forget to vote. They often don't mess with nonvoters unless they think their particular candidate can attract an unusually high number in a certain cohort, such as Obama with young people in 2008. Instead, they focus on the two groups who can get their candidates elected, reliable supporters of their candidate's party and swing voters. The two groups often receive different messages. Supporters are reminded to vote and asked for money. Swings receive a targeted message that in 2012 is probably about jobs or the economy. During early Republican primaries this year, Mitt Romney began sending two sets of national online ads. One, "It's Time to Return American Optimism," was sent to Republicans. In it, Romney called Obama a "pessimistic president" and said this election is one to "save the soul of America." An ad focusing on Romney the family man was sent to undecided voters.[8]

"The people that are going to decide the election is everybody else," said Terry Benham of Little Rock's Impact Management – everybody else being those who aren't committed Republican or Democratic voters. "And everybody else gets broken down into different categories. It's the Walmart women. We've actually started polling that. We've started asking, 'Where do you shop?' in some of our issue polls because we want to know what Walmart women think about a certain issue. ... Those are lower to middle class women. They're pretty independent women. They a lot of times are very opinionated. They're the salt of the earth. They're the salt of the middle ground, and we like to look at that as a demographic and measure that because we think it gives you a really good snapshot of what middle class America is thinking."[9]

How does Impact Management take that snapshot? In Arkansas, certain information is readily available in a public voter file at the secretary of state's office, such as a voter's voting history (when and where they voted and in which party's primary, not who they voted for), birthday, address, some phone numbers, etc. Two miles from the state Capitol is a glass-enclosed mini-skyscraper that is home to Acxiom, one of America's top data processing companies. Acxiom is one of many companies that can provide political consultants with mountains of data about individuals, such as buying habits, whether they have a permit to carry a concealed weapon, and whether they have a hunting license. Once the firm has that information, it conducts a large survey – 3,000 people instead of the usual 300-600 in a poll – looking for anger points and pressure points, intensity of belief, and voters' impression of certain topics such as Obamacare.

To make it all work, campaigns use a mathematical technique known as regression analysis. Once a bunch of middle-income rural Americans who subscribe to Sports Illustrated have told you that they are mad about Obamacare, you can generalize for an entire population: The majority – not all, but the majority – of such people are mad about Obamacare. In fact, there are formulas that determine the odds. And since you know who votes and you have a list of subscribers to Sports Illustrated, you can send just those people a direct mail piece, and you can make sure it's about Obamacare, the issue that is likely to move them. You might even target the advertising very specifically. A pickup truck owner might get a direct mail piece showing a candidate leaning against a truck.[10]

It's fairly basic stuff, actually. Impact's Clint Reed uses Microsoft Excel, which has that as a feature. "Most humans are very habitual about things," Reed said in an interview. "I know I am in terms of where I shop, what I like, the kinds of cars I drive. And really, as you develop that out, what you start doing is you develop probability traits about people. There's the old saying that we used to use in '04: If you drink Bud Light beer and you drive a Chevy truck, chances are you're a Republican. If you drink Mich(elob) Ultra and go to yoga class, you're probably a Democrat. And so it's really developing spending habits, consumer habits, behavioral habits to overlay with voting propensity, how someone may or may not vote. What you do there is, after that, you develop clusters of people: These are swing voters; these are solid Republican voters because they buy Christian magazines and they go to church more than three times a week."[11]

Some of these tendencies make sense, and some don't. If you drive a Volvo, chances are you are a Democrat. Same if you shop at Pottery Barn or have cable TV. If you read various hunting magazines or have satellite television, chances are you are a Republican. Ken Strasma, head of targeting for Obama's 2008 campaign, told Fast Company in October 2008 that polling showed that gin drinkers were more likely to vote Democrat while SUV drivers were more likely to vote Republican.[12]

Likewise, certain regions can be counted on to vote a certain way. It's why we have red states and blue states as well as safe congressional districts and even safe counties. If you live in a county with a Whole Foods grocery store, there is a good chance you are a Democrat. If you live in a county with a Cracker Barrel restaurant, there is a good chance you are a Republican, and those trends are accelerating. In 1992, Bill Clinton won 60 percent of Whole Foods counties and 40 percent of Cracker Barrel counties, a 20 point gap. In 2008, Obama carried 81 percent of counties with a Whole Foods and 36 percent of those with a Cracker Barrel, a 45 percent gap.[13] This makes sense. Cracker Barrels are typically located along interstates in suburban areas. Their Southern-fried meals are more expensive than fast food but still pretty cheap. They brand themselves as a taste of old-fashioned rural life. In other words, they appeal to retirees and upper middle class families who are still on a budget, and those typically are Republicans. Whole Foods offers a selection that is more expensive because it supposedly is environmentally responsible – heaven, in other words, for liberals with money. Those are Democrats.

No, microtargeting won't help campaigns change a lot of made-up minds, but it will alter perceptions, motivate passive partisans and attract swing voters – even those who typically would be inclined to select the other side. A "security mom" might be pro-choice on abortion but also be receptive to Republican anti-terrorism policies. She might get a pro-military direct mail piece from Republicans. Some Christian evangelicals might not support the Democrats' pro-choice stance but do believe the Bible teaches environmental stewardship. A well-crafted piece highlighting a Democratic candidate's green philosophy, while saying nothing about abortion, might attract that voter.[14]

Campaigns are turning more and more to microtargeting for the same reasons that corporations are. Traditional advertising is inefficient, expensive, and filled with pitfalls, including a diffuse audience, ad fatigue and commercial-skipping technology. Campaigns still advertise, of course, and indeed advertising can make the difference in the outcome, as we saw in the 2012 Republican primaries. Mitt Romney simply overwhelmed Rick Santorum and Newt Gingrich on television in certain states because he had almost unlimited resources to define himself and define them while they had limited resources to fight back. But had they had those resources, then the air war would have been a stalemate, and victory would have come elsewhere. The cost of these digital ads is $5 to $9 per thousand households, a much more cost-efficient way of doing business than the typical broadcast TV commercial. It's no wonder that Saul Anuzis, chairman of the Republican National Committee on Technology, told the New York Times in February 2012 that he expected campaigns to spend 10 to 15 percent of their budgets this year on digital political ads.[15]

We're almost finished talking about politics. The final chapter is about personal branding and how you can use the tools we have learned in this book to make yourself more marketable, relevant and influential. Before we go there, however, let's close by asking the question: Is all of this branding, and the technology behind it, good for democracy?

- 13 -

Is Branding Good for Democracy's Brand?

Microtargeting, like all branding techniques, is a tool. It has enabled companies to target their advertising to those consumers who actually want the advertising and might be interested in what the advertiser has to sell. It's how Amazon can let us know that we might like a book and how a supermarket chain can send us coupons for the products we actually buy. Instead of shouting at us Blade Runner-style to get our attention above the din, it enables marketers to touch our shoulder and quietly tell us, often correctly, that we probably would like to buy what they are selling. In politics, it enables campaigns to spread their message using our language while talking about the issues that matter to us. It also lessens the importance of 30-second broadcast television ads that in recent years have provided voters far more heat than light. In the old days, you watched a commercial, usually a negative one, and you were done. Today, you watch an online ad targeted toward your interests and then click on the candidate's website for more information. You then can connect with like-minded voters, turning what has become an observer democracy into more of a participatory one. You might even donate money – always a plus from my perspective as a political fundraiser.

If branding is used to communicate a message succinctly, it is a tool for leadership. Earlier, Impact Management's Terry Benham told us that candidates try to brand entire campaigns so that they are talking about the issues that are important to voters. That's not only appropriate, it's also vital because a campaign is a democratic conversation between candidates and voters, and a conversation isn't possible if neither side cares or knows what the other side is talking about. Ronald Reagan had a brand: less government, lower taxes, strong defense, traditional values. It allowed him to frame the country's complicated problems in a way that inspired and involved busy Americans who might not have a master's degree in macroeconomics but did understand that high taxes plus big government meant a weaker economy, and that the freedom we enjoyed in America was better than the tyranny of communism. At first, an American public that had been raised on the New Deal wasn't particularly receptive, but he continued to present this tightly focused message until eventually his ideas became the foundation for the less government/more government debate that continues today.

On the other hand, if branding is simply a way to react to what's temporarily popular in order to collect more than 50 percent of the votes, then that's an abdication of leadership. Occasionally in American history, progress has come because someone bravely stepped forward in the face of opposition and told people the truth despite it being the opposite of what they wanted to hear. Ending slavery, giving women the right to vote, the civil rights movement – all bucked the tide when first they were introduced. I live in Little Rock, where the nine black students who integrated Central High School in 1957 despite overwhelming public antagonism now are heroes. The governor, Orval Faubus, who then had his finger on the pulse of public opinion, now is the story's villain. Dr. Martin Luther King certainly would not have changed society had he allowed his message to be poll-tested and focus-grouped – though, as a political fundraiser, I can tell you he would have raised a lot more money. "Dr. King," he might have been told, "we need to soften your brand. We like the whole 'I have a dream' message, but this part about black children and white children holding hands in Alabama – that's not going to play with white Southerners above the age of 25. Can you change it to a more general statement about equality? Or maybe just replace 'Alabama' with 'Wisconsin?'"

This could cheapen our elections if misused. The reason that we have all of this voting every two years is so elected officials leave their cocoons and meet a variety of people. It helps ensure that they are accountable to everyone, not just those inclined to vote for them. Thanks to modern campaign technology, candidates can send different pictures of themselves to Cracker Barrel and Whole Foods voters, or, more likely, bypass having any communication with one or the other. That's not encouraging the national conversation that the political process is supposed to be. Remember those town hall meetings when Democrats were confronted by constituents angry over Obamacare? It made them very uncomfortable, which I think our Founding Fathers would have said is a good thing to happen to elected officials every once in a while.

In recent years, we've seen branding taken to extremes in politics. Members of Congress have branded themselves as tea party candidates or friends of MoveOn.org, and that's fine as long as it gives voters an accurate snapshot of what they believe. If it gives candidates a facade to hide behind, however, that's not a good thing. No one doubted that Reagan was a conservative, but he was secure enough in his beliefs, and in his brand, that he was willing to cooperate with Democrats when they could find common ground. These days, Democrats and Republicans are so entrenched in their brands that they can't get anything done – even when they largely agree. What American doesn't think it would be better to obtain energy from homegrown sources than from the places we get it now? Surely Republicans and Democrats could come to some agreement that results in energy independence within 10 years by encouraging both more drilling here and the development of alternative energy sources. Reagan and Speaker of the House Tip O'Neill could have made something happen even though they would have disagreed about degrees of emphasis. Today, however, one side is Coke and one side is Pepsi, and that doesn't leave much room for compromise. Moreover, branding reduces complex problems into slogans and complex people into movie characters. Sen. Marco Rubio of Florida, for example, is so much more than a smart, good-looking Latino Republican, but in a world of branding, that's what some might try to make him. Branding threatens even to reduce the presidency into a commodity, as we saw in 2008, when the election was won by a great brand rather than a qualified candidate. Even presidential vacations have become branding opportunities. When Bill Clinton was in the White House, his advisor, Dick Morris, polled Americans about where he should take a vacation. When a trip to Martha's Vineyard was deemed too elitist, the Clintons instead traveled to Jackson Hole, Wyoming, where the president, a lawyer and career politician, was photographed atop a horse dressed like a cowboy. Ridiculous.

The Constitution opens with the words, "We the people," not "We the brands." If you take nothing else from this book, remember this: People have brands, but people are not brands, and that includes politicians. Today's technology makes it possible – even imperative – that we define ourselves so the marketplace knows what we offer at a glance, but it's the second, deeper look that really matters. Meanwhile, we citizens have a responsibility to look past the brands that are being presented to us by campaigns. Thanks to the internet, a wealth of information is available about candidates if we're willing to spend more than 30 seconds or 140 characters looking for it.

Branding is a tool. We political professionals will do what we do – try to elect the candidates who have hired us and in whom we believe. The voters themselves must decide whether that information helps them make better decisions, or allows them to be manipulated.

- 14 -

What's Your Brand?

As I worked as a national political fundraiser and argued politics on Fox News and CNN, I started realizing that I no longer was just Noelle. I was Noelle Nikpour, strategist, Sun-Sentinel columnist, or whatever tag they were putting beneath my name. I now had a brand that I had to build, maintain and protect.

What's that brand? The kinder, gentler, Southern Ann Coulter. I'm the conservative girl with the accent who doesn't take herself or her politics too seriously. Week after week, I let Obama have it while some liberal from the other side tells me why I'm wrong. We make our points, the host jumps in, we go to commercial, and then my liberal counterpart and I part ways – usually cordially – until it's time to do battle again. No problem.

But other aspects of the role were harder. In addition to raising money for Republican candidates, writing my column, and commenting on television, I'm also a fitness model. I have posed in bathing suits and short sets for magazines and calendars. I do it because I believe in fitness, it brings in income and it reminds me to keep in shape.

Unfortunately, I soon learned that being a fitness model sent a branding signal that was inconsistent with my political and television work. When I started building a fitness website with a picture of myself wearing a two-piece outfit, one media outlet in my hometown of Little Rock prominently featured the picture and pretty much questioned my professional credentials as a fundraiser. I tried very briefly to embrace both sides of my personality, but I quickly realized that I could not as a female argue the conservative point of view on television and then be photographed dressed in a way that could be taken out of context. If I were a liberal, they would probably say I was a free spirit, but I'm neither, so I took down the website and became very choosy about my fitness modeling appearances. Meanwhile, I had another website built for my fundraising and television appearances, www.noelle-nikpour. com, that features a photo of me dressed practically like a nun!

Now that I'm on national television, I know I can never get away from my brand. YOU have a brand, too, whether you want one or not, and you can't get away from yours, either. In fact, it will play a big role in how much success you have in your life.

How did people like you and me get brands? To answer that question, let's look back to 1997. At the time, the economy was humming, the stock market was booming, and money was being made by companies that had few assets besides a web address. While a handful of entrepreneurs were getting rich, most people followed the same path to success their parents had followed: Get their resume ready after high school or college, start interviewing, impress a boss twice their age, and begin climbing the corporate ladder.

But that same year, the author Tom Peters published an article that would herald the start of the personal branding movement. In a piece for Fast Company magazine headlined, "The Brand Called You," he outlined the need for normal people like you and me to brand themselves just as companies branded themselves.

Peters' article would prove to be prophetic. The dot-com bubble burst at the end of the decade, ending the long period of economic growth that had occurred in the 1990s, and the economy has never recovered that momentum. Companies took their jobs to China and replaced factory workers with robots. These days, we're all free agents. If you have a job, there is a good chance it can be outsourced, automated, or made obsolete within five years. Even if it seems secure, you're still competing to keep it against all of those people whose jobs have been outsourced, automated or made obsolete. The Iowa Policy Project estimated in 2005 that 26 percent of all American workers had jobs that were "nonstandard," meaning they were either independent contractors, temps, part-time workers or freelancers. And that was years before the Great Recession had struck.[1]

If you want to remain viable in the workforce, you can mourn the passing of the concept of job security and hope that you can somehow keep making money until you die. Or you can adapt and use the tools that are available today. You can build your brand so that it's there for you even if you lose your job or your business fails. As Penelope Trunk, a career columnist, wrote in The Boston Globe, "In a world where there are no more corporate ladders to land on, your brand is the platform your career will stand on."[2]

Building your brand isn't just helpful; it's necessary. Since everyone is a free agent, you must be able to sell yourself. If you own your own business, you have no choice. People are not going to come just because you build it. If you're looking for a job, it can be the attribute that differentiates you from your competitors. As personal branding expert Dan Schawbel explained in his book "Me 2.0," "A decade ago, if you met someone, you would have no idea whom they knew and how many people they were connected to. Those days are over. Soon, your network will be the only differentiator, when all expertise is equal. The size, activity rate, and reach of your network is becoming a job qualification, especially in this competitive environment. Best Buy posted a job listing at its website with a requirement of 250+ Twitter followers. If you were a hiring manager and you stumbled upon two qualified applicants with the same background, but one had 500 contacts while the other had 5, whom would you hire? Exactly. Your network matters now more than ever."[3]

So how do you build your brand? The first step is to ask yourself four questions: What are my qualities? What are my goals? How do others see me? How do I want them to see me?

Honesty is the key here because your personal branding must match the person you are. If you're not sure how to start, describe yourself to someone else, and be accurate. Don't create a television character or a corporate cartoon spokesperson for yourself. Be real, because people gravitate toward authenticity. They want truth, not just "that which is true." I'm not being touchy-feely here. "That which is true" is a technicality and can be as deceptive as a lie. It's, "I did not have sexual relationships with that woman, Miss Lewinsky," which, I guess, was factually true word by word but did not communicate the truth. If you try to be something you are not, you will fail – first, because you will be found out, and second, because you'll create the conflict and stress in your life that is common to all phonies and hypocrites. If you have branded yourself a church attender for whatever reasons, including very good ones, then you need to be prepared to toss or sell every low-cut blouse you own. If your idea of a good time is staying at home to watch a "Star Trek" marathon, don't brand yourself a partier. In other words, be yourself. Don't be Michael Dukakis driving around in a tank. As Harry and Christine Beckwith wrote in their excellent 2007 book, "You, Inc.," "We buy how good you are. But assuming you are among several candidates whom we consider capable, we buy not how good you are at what you do. We buy how good you are at who you are."[4] Be authentic. Be real. And the market will reward you for it.

Authenticity works. It's why Ronald Reagan had that famous "Teflon brand." His opponents in politics and the media never could figure out why the missteps that would have stuck permanently to other politicians seemed to slide off him like butter on a Teflon-coated pan. Americans knew he wasn't perfect. They knew he had to compromise to get anything done. But they also knew that he truly believed what he was saying, that he truly loved his country, and that his seeming inconsistencies were the result of circumstance or human error and not because of malicious intent or failures of character.

Being honest and accurate, however, does give you the freedom to present the best you possible, and the best you is not the one you are now but the one you are trying to be. That's what having goals is all about. Paint a picture – actually, a better version of yourself than exists now, but one that's true and attainable. In other words, while you are creating and building your brand, make sure it will take you somewhere you want to go. Meanwhile, be aware that your associations, particularly your employer, can brand you. If you work for a tobacco company or for a government official you no longer agree with, then you need to minimize that association until you can get out of it. Separate your business and personal life where you can, such as your Twitter and Facebook pages, and then rebrand yourself in those places as you move toward a different life. As Dan Schawbel explained in an interview for this book, "The key is you want to brand yourself in the career you want, not the job you have. That's the key. Then you're going to attract the right opportunities and repel the ones that are not a good fit. For instance, if you hate your job, but all over the 'net, it shows that you're an employee of that company and that you're doing certain work there, you're never going to get the job that you want. You're just going to keep getting recruited for jobs that are reflective of the current job you have. So that's why you have to tailor your online presence to attract the opportunity that you really want."[5]

Remember what we learned earlier in the book: You can't just be good, and it's not even enough to be better. You have to be different. I would not be appearing on national television if they couldn't put the words "Republican Party strategist" after my name and if I didn't have this Southern accent. If there were already a conservative commentator who looked like me and sounded like me and did what I do, Fox News and other networks wouldn't have given me a second look.

As you consider your qualities, determine where you add value. You are selling yourself, so what are you asking people to buy? If you want your brand to matter, then you have to be an authority on something, which means finding your niche in a particular area that you can make yours. You want to be the person to whom people look for answers in your particular area of expertise. As Nikolas Allen, who owns BAM! Small Biz Consulting, wrote in Personal Branding magazine, "One mistake many people make is trying to be everything to everybody. Having many interests is understandable, especially early in your life or career. However, branding yourself as 'jack of all trades' does not create a perception of 'multi-talented flexibility'; it only creates the perception of 'unfocused amateur.'"[6]

Learn from the people and the companies that have successfully branded themselves. Dan Schawbel was a painfully shy kid, but then he made himself into in the media's go-to guy when it came to questions about personal branding among the millennial generation. He created a niche for himself and then filled it. You can do that in your field. FedEx branded itself as the company to call "when it absolutely, positively has to be there overnight." Can you be the person to call when someone needs the services you offer on an impossibly tight deadline? Nordstrom has made a name for itself by offering almost over the top customer service. Will you go the extra mile for a client?

You don't have to be famous. Dan Schawbel isn't. You just have to be connected to the people who can help you achieve your goals. For many of us, it's more important to market ourselves very effectively to 50 people than it is to be vaguely familiar to 50 million. It's unlikely that you are ever going to own a concept in the marketplace like Kleenex owns tissue paper. You just won't have that kind of marketing budget. But it's probably not necessary for that to happen. The goal here is micro-fame; being well-known where you need to be well-known. According to Schawbel, "A lot of people try to be everything to everyone, and it's just really ineffective. The best strategy is always to go for a specific audience so that you can tailor your expertise to that audience, you can really become the master of your domain, and people will seek you out."[7]

How do others see you, and how do you want them to see you? This is where the tools of branding come into play. The first step is to define yourself, remembering that brevity is not just necessary but mandatory. Remember Clare Booth Luce's comment, "A great man is one sentence"? You're probably not yet great, and you don't get a sentence. According to Schawbel, "I would say it's no more than five words because after that people forget."[8]

Your sentence, your headline, positions you in the marketplace, and then you can use various communication techniques to flesh it out. The most important of those has existed as long as mankind has sat around a campfire: the art of storytelling, because stories are how we understand the world. How do you tell your story? You do it by using offline tools such as your various activities, professional and personal, where people see you and your work in person, and by using online tools including a website, a blog, Facebook and LinkedIn pages and a Twitter account. These are free or very cheap.

In fact, you do not need an enormous budget to market yourself. Starbucks and Walmart grew to dominate their industries despite spending very little on advertising. Instead, you need to offer value to the marketplace and be different enough that your micro-fame will spread. However, remember that your story must be your own. Don't try to make yourself into some literary archetype. Remember the advertising slogan for the original "Superman" movie: "You will believe a man can fly"? Real people eventually come back down to earth. In fact, the best brands are the ones that make the audience, not the product, the hero. Good examples are Apple and Nike, whose highly aspirational marketing efforts inspire rather than simply convince customers to buy their products.

Of course, there is a good chance you already are doing these things, but you may not be doing them effectively. Dan Schawbel says branding has to be a habit like brushing your teeth because it's that important. Online, that means posting regularly and keeping your profiles up to date. He recommends focusing on one social media tool; he personally likes Facebook because of its algorithm and popularity. As for your website, you must make sure you appear high on search engines. You know the old saying, "It's not what you know but who you know"? These days it's, "It's not what you know, it's how well Google knows you." If you aren't on the first two or three pages, you don't exist online. Concentrate on a few keywords or a keyword catchphrase that will move you up the list. Conduct a search for words associated with your niche and then study the pages that appear high in the search engine and are similar to yours. Google likes the ones that appear up top.[9] You'll also want to make sure your online platforms showcase your brand in the best possible way, so that means taking advantage of audio, video and other tools. Got a YouTube account? Consider getting one. It's not just for consuming video and wasting time; it also is a powerful branding tool.

Online, the best way to receive is first to give. Much of the internet's economy is based on sellers giving away products and content for free in order to entice people to stay long enough to buy something. Peter Shankman, founder of the company "Help a Reporter Out," which connects reporters to sources, explained that philosophy in an interview published in the August 2011 issue of Personal Branding magazine. "Well, it was never advertised," he said. "Essentially, what I did was I created something that people saw as helpful and free; helpful and free are probably the two best things you can do in the world because helpful and free help you create your brand."[10]

Remember that you and your brand are inseparable. Whatever you do in the real world can be photographed and recorded and remembered by somebody. Whatever you post online can be seen by anybody and will never go away, so treat it like it might be read by your grandmother, your wife, your children and, someday, your grandchildren. That hard lesson ended the promising career of the ironically named New York Democrat, Rep. Anthony Weiner, who decided it would be a good idea to send a picture of his crotch to a young woman who is not his wife via Twitter. He became a national laughingstock and resigned from office.

Don't be a Weiner. All publicity is not good publicity. While most of us aren't marginally famous congressmen with mockable names, we do have online reputations that can be permanently damaged thanks to a thoughtless post on Facebook or Twitter. Teachers get drummed out of their profession when their inappropriate Facebook relationships become public. In my home state of Arkansas, a school board member was forced to resign from office after he made a harsh anti-gay comment on Facebook that made national news. Employers now routinely check applicants' Facebook pages and won't hire those who could prove embarrassing. According to ExecuNet, 90 percent of recruiters use a search engine to research potential employees and 46 percent have eliminated candidates because of what they learned.[11] The online chain of evidence that follows us everywhere we go has even changed the way we find a mate, and not just through online dating sites such as eHarmony. As Schawbel wrote in his book "Me 2.0," "There's no such thing as even a blind date anymore. You can just Facebook your prospective companion's name and decide whether to go out or not, based on appearance and how that person behaves online. Most of the time, you won't even meet someone offline, so online impressions have become a very powerful force."[12]

As you build your brand, don't make the same mistake that so many companies have made in trying to force-feed your audience a version of yourself. One of the great strengths of the internet is that it allows two-way communication. Listen. Use the internet and social media as a way to have a conversation rather than simply give a speech. Read the comments you receive as a result of your posts on your blog, Facebook and Twitter. And then use those comments to improve your brand. That doesn't mean you stick your finger in the air to see what direction the wind is blowing. It means you take advantage of the wisdom of the crowds to modify, redirect and change your emphasis.

Branding is a fancy word for communication, and that's all you're trying to do: communicate that you have something to offer so that people will give you one of the most valuable things they own, their attention. Then you can persuade them to give you something else that's valuable to you: their money, their vote, whatever.

Communication, as you may have noticed, is hard. Whatever you say must be simple and brief. I'm reasonably well informed about a lot of things, but I'm only an expert in one thing, and that's raising money for Republican candidates. But, in a three-minute segment on national television, I can outdebate a Ph.D. in his own field because while I'm hammering home one simple fact, he's trying to explore the big picture in all its nuances. That works at academic conferences. I wish it would work in the Congress. But on television and on the internet, it doesn't work. As Chip and Dan Heath wrote in their excellent 2007 book, "Made to Stick," "Concrete language helps people, especially novices, understand new concepts. Abstraction is the luxury of the expert."[13]

Once we know a fact, it's hard for us to imagine others not knowing it, so don't assume that people know what you know or understand what you are trying to communicate. In 1990, doctoral candidate Elizabeth Newton conducted a study in which she had individual subjects tap out the notes to songs with their knuckles while individual listeners tried to guess what they were playing. When asked, the tappers in her study figured that the listeners would correctly guess the song about half the time. It turned out that, out of 120 songs, the listeners guessed only two. The reason is that the tappers could hear the notes to the songs in their heads, while the listeners only heard a rhythmic tapping. Try it, and then remember it the next time you are trying to communicate a concept to someone who knows less about the subject than you do.

Other tips for building a brand? It's helpful to have a memorable and marketable name, especially one that can rise above the internet clutter.[14] Your email address is important, too, so don't have one with a bunch of numbers and abbreviations unless you are trying to make it hard for people to remember you. Ivana Taylor, who writes the marketing strategy blog "Strategy Stew," recommends adopting a "physical trigger" to make yourself memorable – think Steve Jobs' turtlenecks or the white suits that KFC's Col. Harlan Sanders always wore. She also advised creating catch-phrases that can be associated with you.[15] Be patient. Your brand is a relationship between you and your audience, and any relationship takes time to develop.

Finally, remember this: A 2008 Duke University study found that it's easier to remember someone's name when they smile because the brain's orbitofrontal cortex, the part associated with reward processing, is more active then.[16]

So smile. It's good for your brand!

Notes

CHAPTER ONE

1   Ogunnaike, Lola; "Paris Inc."; The New York Times; May 2, 2005; http://www.nytimes.com/2005/05/02/arts/02pari.html

2   Ibid

3   Ibid

4   Marikar, Shelia; "Kim Kardashian's Mom: No Money Made From Wedding"; ABC News website; Nov. 2, 2011; http://abcnews.go.com/blogs/entertainment/2011/11/kim-kardashian-i-would-never-marry-for-money/

5   Iyer, Pico; "America's First Renaissance Woman: Clare Booth Luce: 1903-1987"; Time magazine; Oct. 19, 1987; http://www.time.com/time/magazine/article/0,9171,965754,00.html

6   Noonan, Peggy; "To-do List: A Sentence, Not 10 Paragraphs"; The Wall Street Journal; June 26, 2009; http://online.wsj.com/article/SB124596573543456401.html

CHAPTER TWO

1   Klaassen, Abbey; "New Coke: One of marketing biggest blunders turn 25"; Advertising Age; April 23, 2010; http://adage.com/article/adages/coke-marketing-s-biggest-blunders-turns-25/143470/

2   Lindstrom, Martin; "Buyology"; Doubleday; New York; 2008; pages 99-101, 124-125

3   Interbrand website; http://www.interbrand.com/en/best-global-brands/best-global-brands-2008/best-global-brands-2011.aspx

4   Adamson, Allen; "BrandSimple"; Palgrave MacMillan; New York; 2006

5   Conley, Lucas; "Obsessive Branding Disorder"; PublicAffairs; New York; 2008; page 3

6   Margenau, Scott; "What is Branding? What's the Difference Between Marketing and Branding? A New Look at an Old Debate."; July 8, 2011; http://www.imageworksstudio.com/blog/what-branding-whats-difference-between-marketing-and-branding-new-look-old-debate/index.html

7   Adamson, Allen; "BrandSimple"; Palgrave MacMillan; New York; 2006; page 6

8   Adamson, pages xvi-xvii

9   Adamson, page 12

10   Motel 6 website; http://www.motel6.com/about/corpprofile.aspx

11 Williams, Kimberly; "Actually, Motel 6 Doesn't Leave the Light on for You"; AdvertisingAge; Aug. 30, 2007; http://adage.com/article/news/motel-6-leave-light/120172/

12 Adamson, page 29

13 Lindstrom, Martin; "Buyology"; Doubleday; New York; 2008; pages 37-38

14 Story, Louise; "Anywhere the eye can see, it's likely to see an ad"; The New York Times; January 15, 2007; http://www.nytimes.com/2007/01/15/business/media/15everywhere.html?pagewanted=all

15 Conley, page 11

16 Gupta, Nitin; "Will Social Media lead to the demise of Google"; Digital Marketing Today; Sept. 28, 2009; http://digitalmarketingtoday.com/2009/09/28/will-social-media-lead-to-the-demise-of-google/

17 Flint, Joe; "Ad-skip feature irks big players"; Los Angeles Times; printed in the Arkansas Democrat-Gazette; May 16, 2012

18 Nielsen; nielsen.com

19 Lindstrom, Martin; "Brandwashed: Tricks Companies Use to Manipulate Our Minds and Persuade Us to Buy"; Random House, Inc.; Kindle Edition; Sept. 20, 2011; locations 525-532, 1275-1278

20 "Global Advertising: Consumers Trust Real Friends and Virtual Strangers the Most"; Nielsen Wire; July 7, 2009; http://blog.nielsen.com/nielsenwire/consumer/global-advertising-consumers-trust-real-friends-and-virtual-strangers-the-most/

21 Keller, Ed and Fay, Brad; "The Face-to-Face Book"; Simon & Schuster, Inc.; Kindle Edition; May 22, 2012; locations 1860-1864

22 Keller, Ed and Berry, Jon; "The Influentials"; Free Press; 2003

23 Gladwell, Malcolm; "The Tipping Point"; Little, Brown and Company; New York; 2002; pages 3-5

24 Lindstrom, Martin; "Brandwashed: Tricks Companies Use to Manipulate Our Minds and Persuade Us to Buy"; Random House, Inc.; Kindle Edition; Sept. 20, 2011; locations 2102-2109, 2158-2171, 2314-2322, 2331-2340, 2355-2361, 2371-2383

25 Storey, Louise: "Product packages now shout to get your attention'"; The New York Times; August 10, 2007; http://www.nytimes.com/2007/08/10/business/10package.html

26 "Buyology"; pages 141-151, 156-158

27 Conley; pages 134-139, 141-143, 165-169

28 Gobe, Marc; "Emotional Branding, Revised Edition: The New Paradigm for Connecting Brands to People"; Allworth Press; Kindle Edition; April 22, 2010; locations 2246-2250

CHAPTER THREE

1   Conley, Lucas; "Obsessive Branding Disorder"; PublicAffairs; New York; 2008; page 3

2   Lindstrom, Martin; "Buyology"; Doubleday; New York; 2008; pages 26-27

3   Lindstrom, Martin; "Brandwashed: Tricks Companies Use to Manipulate Our Minds and Persuade Us to Buy"; Random House, Inc.; Kindle Edition; Sept. 20, 2011; locations 3901-3903

4   Adamson, Allen; "BrandSimple"; Palgrave MacMillan; New York; 2006; page 14, 19, 36

5   Mathieson, Rick; "The On-Demand Brand"; American Management Association; New York; 2010; pages 4-7

6   "Brandwashed"; locations 2421-2425, 2677-2693

7   "Brandwashed," locations 783-785

8   "Brandwashed"; locations 769-773, 796-799, 845-853

9   "Brandwashed"; locations 722-730, 740-753

10   "Bowling Alone"; bowlingalone.com

11   Conley, Lucas; "Obsessive Branding Disorder"; PublicAffairs; New York; 2008; page 78-81

12   "Apple iTunes Intro - Part 1"; YouTube video uploaded by delll1032; May 29, 2007

13   "Apple iTunes Intro - Part 2"; YouTube video uploaded by delll1032; May 29, 2007

14   "Apple Music Event 2003 - iTunes Music Store Introduction"; YouTube uploaded by peestandingup; Nov. 8, 2007

15   Crum, Rex; "Apple tops Microsoft on S&P 500, index's guardian says"; Marketwatch; April 22, 2010; http://articles.marketwatch.com/2010-04-22/industries/30744667_1_microsoft-shares-apple-shares-s-p

16   Ovide, Shira; "Will Tim Cook Free Apple's Cash Stockpile"; "Deal Journal"; Wall Street Journal website; Nov. 1, 2011; http://blogs.wsj.com/deals/2011/11/01/will-tim-cook-free-apples-cash-stockpile/

CHAPTER FOUR

1   Bennett, Shea; "Twitter On Track for 500 Million Total Users by March, 250 Million Active Users By End of 2012"; mediabistro; Jan. 13, 2012; http://www.mediabistro.com/alltwitter/twitter-active-total-users_b17655

2   Lindstrom, Martin; "Brandwashed: Tricks Companies Use to Manipulate Our Minds and Persuade Us to Buy"; Random House, Inc.; Kindle Edition; Sept. 20, 2011; locations 2355-2361, 2371-2383

3   Bennett, Shea; "Twitter On Track for 500 Million Total Users by
        March, 250 Million Active Users By End of 2012"; mediabistro;
        Jan. 13, 2012; http://www.mediabistro.com/alltwitter/twitter-active-
        total-users_b17655

4   Walsh, Mark; "Facebook CPMs Climb Despite Falling Clicks";
        Online Media Daily; April 16, 2012; http://www.mediapost.com/
        publications/article/172447/facebook-cpms-climb-despite-falling-
        clicks.html

5   Bennett, Shea; "Twitter Ad Revenue Tipped to Reach $540 Million
        by 2014 [Report]"; All Twitter; Jan. 31, 2012; http://www.media-
        bistro.com/alltwitter/twitter-ad-revenue-2014_b18138

6   Schawbel, Dan"; "Me 2.0, Revised and Updated Edition: 4 Steps
        to Building Your Future"; Kaplan; Kindle Edition; Feb. 20, 2011;
        locations 2305-2313

7   Mathieson, Rick; "The On-Demand Brand"; American Management
        Association; New York; 2010; page 63

8   Goldhaber, Michael; "The Attention Economy and the Net"; First
        Monday; Volume 2, Number 4; April 7, 1997; http://firstmonday.org/
        article/view/519/440

9   Goldhaber, Michael; "Attention Shoppers!"; Wired; December 1997;
        http://www.wired.com/wired/archive/5.12/es_attention.html

10   Trout, Jack; "Big Brands Big Trouble"; John Wiley and Sons, Inc.;
        New York; 2001; page 19

11   Gregory, Sean; "Domino's YouTube Crisis: 5 Ways to Fight Back";
        Time; April 18, 2009; http://www.time.com/time/nation/
        article/0,8599,1892389,00.html

12   Ibid

13   Clifford, Stephanie; "Video Prank at Domino's Taints Brand"; The
        New York Times; April 15, 2009; http://www.nytimes.com/2009/
        04/16/business/media/16dominos.html

14   FedEx website; http://blog.fedex.designcdt.com/absolutely-
        positively-unacceptable?page=1

15   Neff, Jack; "Lever's CMO Throws Down the Social-Media Gauntlet";
        Advertising Age; April 13, 2009; http://adage.com/article/digital/
        unilever-cmo-clift-throws-social-media-gauntlet/135943/

CHAPTER FIVE

1   "Privacy Policy"; Apple website; http://www.apple.com/privacy/; last
        updated May 21, 2012

2   Lindstrom, Martin; "Brandwashed: Tricks Companies Use to
        Manipulate Our Minds and Persuade Us to Buy"; Random
        House, Inc.; Kindle Edition; Sept. 20, 2011; locations 4099-4109

3   Katsaras, Nikolaos; Wolfson, Paul; Kinsey, Jean; Senauer, Ben; "Data Mining: A Segmentation Analysis of U.S. Grocery Shoppers; Department of Applied Economics; University of Minnesota; March 2001; http://ageconsearch.umn.edu/handle/14335

4   Lindstrom, Martin; "Buyology"; Doubleday; New York; 2008; pages 14-15

5   "Brandwashed"; locations 4440-4483

6   Angwin, Julia; "Latest in web tracking: Stealthy 'Supercookies'"; Wall Street Journal; August 19, 2011; http://online.wsj.com/article/SB10001424053111903480904576508382675931492.html

7   "Brandwashed"; locations 4153-4161

8   Duhigg, Charles; "How companies learn your secrets"; New York Times; Feb. 16, 2012; http://www.nytimes.com/2012/02/19/magazine/shopping-habits.html?pagewanted=all

9   Ibid

10   Brickstream, www.brickstream.com

11   Sorensen, Herb, Ph.D.; "The Three Faces of PathTracker"; TNSglobal.com blog; June 3, 2009; http://blogs.tnsglobal.com/retail_shopper/2009/06/the-three-faces-of-pathtracker-.html

12   Sorensen, Herb, Ph.D.; "Inside the Mind of a Shopper"; Wharton School Publishing; Upper Saddle River, New Jersey; 2009

13   "Brandwashed"; locations 4633-4637

14   Siegler, M.G.; "Eric Schmidt: Every 2 Days We Create As Much Information As We Did Up To 2003"; TechCrunch; 2010; http://techcrunch.com/2010/08/04/schmidt-data/

15   "Google CEO Eric Schmidt on privacy";YouTube video uploaded by theyTOLDyou on Dec. 8, 2009; http://www.youtube.com/watch?v=A6e7wfDHzew

16   Graham, Bob; Daily Mail; Daily Mail online; "George Orwell, Big Brother is watching your house"; March 31, 2007; http://www.dailymail.co.uk/news/article-445897/George-Orwell-Big-Brother-watching-house.html

17   "Privacy Policy"; Apple website; http://www.apple.com/privacy/; last updated May 21, 2012

CHAPTER SIX

1   Interview with Terry Benham, March 2012

2   Brock, Roby; "Same-sex Marriage Unpopular with Fourth District Democrats and Republicans"; talkbusiness.net; May 10, 2012; http://talkbusiness.net/2012/05/same-sex-marriage-unpopular-with-fourth-district-democrats-and-republicans/

3   Interview with Terry Benham, March 2012

4   Heilemann, John and Halperin, Mark; "Game Change: Obama and the Clintons, McCain and Palin, and the Race of a Lifetime"; HarperCollins e-books; Kindle Edition; Feb. 9, 2010; page 386

5   Interview with Terry Benham, March 2012

6   Smith, Steve; "Exclusive: Agony of TV teenager filmed sneering during Susan Boyle's debut"; Daily Record; www.dailyrecord.co.uk; Nov. 22, 2009; http://www.dailyrecord.co.uk/news/real-life/2009/11/22/exclusive-agony-of-tv-teenager-filmed-sneering-during-susan-boyle-s-debut-86908-21841022/

7   Bernstein, "The Speech"; Chicago Magazine; June 2007; http://www.chicagomag.com/Chicago-Magazine/June-2007/The-Speech/

8   Kelling, George; "How New York Became Safe: The Full Story"; City Journal; July 1, 2009

9   Kelling, George; "The Mounting Evidence that Broken Windows Works"; City Journal; July 1, 2009

10   Pooley, Eric; "Mayor of the World"; Time; Dec. 31, 2001; http://www.time.com/time/specials/packages/article/0,28804,2020227_2020306_2022358,00.html

11   Benen, Steve; "High Infidelity"; Washington Monthly; July/August 2006

12   "9/11 News Coverage: 2:38 PM: Giuliani-Pataki Press Conference"; YouTube video uploaded by Authentic History on Jan. 30, 2011; http://www.youtube.com/watch?v=xhBYWDy4m9M

13   "Mayor of the World"; Time; Dec. 31, 2001

14   Ibid

15   Ibid

CHAPTER SEVEN

1   Smithsonian Institute's National Museum of American History; http://americanhistory.si.edu/exhibitions/small_exhibition.cfm?key=1267&exkey=696&pagekey=701

2   Chicago History Museum; http://blog.chicagohistory.org/index.php/2009/11/the-railsplitter/

3   Flexner, James Thomas; "Washington The Indispensable Man"; New American Library; New York; 1974

4   McNamara, Robert; "The 1840 Presidential Election"; About.com; http://history1800s.about.com/od/leaders/a/1840campaign.htm

5   McNamara, Robert; "The election of 1884 between Cleveland and Blaine was marked by scandals"; About.com; http://history1800s.about.com/od/presidentialcampaigns/a/electionof1884.htm

6   "Nixon's famous Checkers speech turns 50"; The Nixon Era Times; Official Publication of the Nixon Era Center at Mountain State University; http://www.nixonera.com/

7   American Rhetoric; americanrhetoric.com; "Richard M. Nixon –
        'Checkers'"; http://www.americanrhetoric.com/speeches/
        richardnixoncheckers.html
8   "President Kennedy's Health Secrets"; PBS NewsHour; transcript
        of interview by Ray Suarez of Dr. Jeffrey Kelman; http://www.pbs.
        org/newshour/bb/health/july-dec02/jfk_11-18.html
9   "Lyndon Johnson - Daisy"; YouTube video uploaded by 10usc311 on
        Oct. 18, 2006
10   "George Romney Brainwash interview on WKBD-TV 50"; YouTube
        video uploaded by p1harw66 on June 4, 2008; http://www.youtube.
        com/watch?v=fSdSiBehQpI
11   Ries, Al and Trout, Jack; "The 22 Immutable Laws of Marketing";
        Harper Collins, Inc.; Kindle Edition; Oct. 13, 2009; locations 824-
        825
12   Ries and Trout, locations 847-853
13   Choi, Candice; "Domino's says 'No" to customers in latest TV ad";
        Associated Press; published on usatoday.com; April 3, 2012; http://
        www.usatoday.com/money/industries/food/story/2012-04-03/
        dominos-pizza-ad-no/53968482/1
14   "Bill Clinton 60 Minutes Interview 1992 ElectionWallDotOrg.flv";
        http://www.youtube.com/watch?v=BF9LJw20bSc
        YouTube video uploaded by electionwalldot.org on June 9, 2011
15   Ibid

CHAPTER EIGHT
1   Will Rogers Today website; http://www.willrogerstoday.com/
        will_rogers_quotes/quotes.cfm?qID=4
2   "Ronald Reagan .. 'Government is the problem'"; YouTube recording
        of Reagan inaugural address uploaded by rickeypickles on Oct. 20,
        2009; http://www.youtube.com/watch?v=XObcP69dhCg
3   Ries, Al and Trout, Jack; "The 22 Immutable Laws of Marketing";
        Harper Collins, Inc.; Kindle Edition; Oct. 13, 2009; location789
4   "Obama: GOP is the party of ideas for the last 10-15 years"; YouTube
        video of Obama remarks uploaded by tryl8 on Jan. 17, 2008; http://
        www.youtube.com/watch?v=mbaszmcpesc
5   "Obama: Reagan changed direction; Bill Clinton didn't"; YouTube
        video uploaded by Veracifier on Jan. 21, 2008; http://www.youtube.
        com/watch?v=HFLuOBsNMZA
6   Ries, Al and Trout, Jack; "The 22 Immutable Laws of Marketing";
        Harper Collins, Inc.; Kindle Edition; Oct. 13, 2009; locations 74-111
7   "Sir Roger Bannister"; Academy of Achievement website; www.
        achievement.org; http://www.achievement.org/autodoc/
        page/ban0bio-1/

8 Trout, Jack; "Big Brands Big Trouble"; John Wiley and Sons, Inc.; New York; 2001; page 32

9 Geldof, Bob; "Geldof and Bush: Diary from the Road"; Time; Feb. 28, 2008; http://www.time.com/time/world/article/0,8599,1717934,00.html

10 Ries and Trout, locations 859-874

11 "Hispanics increasing Catholic numbers in US, but assimilation has downside"; Catholic News Agency; March 17, 2010; http://www.catholicnewsagency.com/news/hispanics_increasing_catholic_numbers_in_us_but_assimilation_has_downside/

12 Lopez, Mark; "The Latino Vote in the 2010 Elections"; Pew Research Center; Nov. 3, 2010; http://www.pewhispanic.org/2010/11/03/the-latino-vote-in-the-2010-elections/

13 Ries and Trout, locations 349-350

14 Mendes, Elizabeth; Gallup website; "In U.S., fear of big government at near-record level: survey dated Dec. 12, 2011"; http://www.gallup.com/poll/151490/fear-big-government-near-record-level.aspx

15 Ries and Trout; locations 192-194, 346-347

16 Ries and Trout, locations 813-822

17 Ries and Trout, locations 1214-1221

18 Green, Joshua; "Reagan's Liberal Legacy"; Washington Monthly; January/February 2003; http://www.washingtonmonthly.com/features/2001/0301.green.html

19 Ries and Trout, locations 2051-2062

CHAPTER NINE

1 Heilemann, John and Halperin, Mark; "Game Change: Obama and the Clintons, McCain and Palin, and the Race of a Lifetime"; HarperCollins e-books; Kindle Edition; Feb. 9, 2010; pages 43, 51, 88

2 Johnson, Haynes and Balz, Dan; "The Battle for America: The Story of an Extraordinary Election"; Kindle Edition; Penguin; July 23, 2009; locations 492-500

3 Johnson and Balz, locations 561-580

4 Heilemann and Halperin; pages 67-68, 73, 136

5 Johnson and Balz; locations 882-889

6 Heilemann and Halperin; pages 92, 98-99

7 McGirt, Ellen; "The Brand Called Obama"; Fast Company; April 1, 2008; http://www.fastcompany.com/magazine/124/the-brand-called-obama.html

8 "Sol Sender Part 1: Creating an Identity for the Obama Campaign"; YouTube video uploaded by University of Oklahoma on Oct. 12, 2010; http://www.youtube.com/watch?v=51zmylaqCBQ

9   "Sol Sender – Obama Logo Design Part 1 of 2"; YouTube video
        uploaded by VSA Partners on Dec. 22, 2008; http://www.youtube.
        com/watch?v=etEP1Bhgui0

10   "Sol Sender Part 2: The Evolution of the Logo"; YouTube video
        uploaded by University of Oklahoma on Oct. 12, 2010; http://www.
        youtube.com/watch?v=prWeQu7pQsM

11   "Sol Sender – Obama Logo Design Part 1 of 2"

12   "Sol Sender Part 2: The Evolution of the Logo"

13   "Designing Obama"; YouTube video uploaded by Walker Art
        Center on May 18, 2009; http://www.youtube.com/
        watch?v=keZlITOpY3k

14   Romano, Andrew; "Expertinent: Why the Obama 'brand' is
        working"; Newsweek; Feb. 27, 2008; http://www.thedailybeast.com/
        newsweek/blogs/stumper/2008/02/27/expertinent-why-the-obama-
        quot-brand-quot-is-working.html

15   "Designing Obama"

16   McGirt, Ellen, "The Brand Called Obama"

17   Ibid

18   Ibid

19   "Sol Sender Part 2: The Evolution of the Logo"

20   Romano, Andrew; "Expertinent: Why the Obama 'brand' is
        working"

21   Heilemann and Halperin, pages 161-162

22   Johnson and Balz, locations 1571-1607

23   Heilemann and Halperin, page 281

24   McGirt, Ellen, "The Brand Called Obama"

25   Johnson and Balz, locations 2205-2217

26   Heilemann and Halperin, pages 291-295

27   Heilemann and Halperin, page 306

28   Heilemann and Halperin; pages 314-346

29   Heilemann and Halperin; pages 354-373

30   Ross, Brian; "Obama's Pastor: God Damn America, U.S. to Blame
        for 9/11"; ABC News; March 13, 2008; http://abcnews.go.com/
        Blotter/DemocraticDebate/story?id=4443788&page=1#.T_
        r6LGg5jOE

31   The Huffington Post; "Obama Race Speech: Read the Full Text";
        Huffington Post; March 18, 2008; http://www.huffingtonpost.
        com/2008/03/18/obama-race-speech-read-th_n_92077.html

32   Heilemann and Halperin; pages 395-398

33   "Michelle Obama: 'For the first time in my adult lifetime, I'm really
        proud of my country'"; ABC News; Feb. 18, 2008; http://abcnews.
        go.com/blogs/politics/2008/02/michelle-obam-1-2/

34   Heilemann and Halperin; page 386

35   Heilemann and Halperin; page 387
36   "Obama rues 'bitter' remark"; BBC News; April 12, 2008; http://
        news.bbc.co.uk/2/hi/7344532.stm
37   Heilemann and Halperin; page 421

CHAPTER TEN

1   Johnson, Haynes and Balz, Dan. "The Battle for America: The Story
        of an Extraordinary Election"; Penguin; Kindle Edition; July 23,
        2009; locations 4876-4880
2   Madden, Mike; "Inside the Campaign Ad Machine"; Adweek; June
        27, 2011; http://www.adweek.com/news/advertising-branding/
        inside-campaign-ad-machine-132898
3   Heilemann, John and Halperin, Mark; "Game Change: Obama and
        the Clintons, McCain and Palin, and the Race of a Lifetime";
        HarperCollins e-books; Kindle Edition; Feb. 9, 2010; pages 527-528
4   Heilemann and Halperin; pages 529-530, 536
5   Heilemann and Halperin, page 598
6   Dannen, Chris; "How Obama Won It with the Web"; Fast Company;
        Nov. 4 2008; http://www.fastcompany.com/articles/2008/11/how-
        obama-won-it-with-the-web.html?page=0%2C1
7   Ibid
8   Keller, Ed and Fay, Brad; "The Face-to-Face Book"; Simon &
        Schuster, Inc.; Kindle Edition; May 22, 2012; locations 1103-1119
9   Keller and Fay, locations 1125-1157
10   Heilemann and Halperin, pages 609-610
11   Creamer, Matthew; "Obama Wins! ... Ad Age's Marketer of the
        Year"; Advertising Age; Oct. 17, 2008; http://adage.com/article/
        moy-2008/obama-wins-ad-age-s-marketer-year/131810/
12   Ries, Al; "What Marketers Can Learn from Obama's Campaign";
        Advertising Age; Nov. 5, 2008; http://adage.com/article/al-ries/
        marketers-learn-obama-s-campaign/132237/
13   Ibid
14   Klein, Naomi; "Naomi Klein on how corporate branding has taken
        over America"; The Guardian; January 15, 2010; http://www.
        guardian.co.uk/books/2010/jan/16/naomi-klein-branding-obama-
        america

CHAPTER ELEVEN

1   Center for American Women and Politics; "Women in the U.S.
        Congress 2012"; http://www.cawp.rutgers.edu/fast_facts/levels_of_
        office/documents/cong.pdf

2 Center for American Women and Politics; "Statewide Elected Executive Women"; http://www.cawp.rutgers.edu/fast_facts/levels_ of_office/documents/stwide.pdf

3 Memo written by Rep. Cathy McMorris Rogers to interested parties; Nov. 18, 2010

4 Center for American Women and Politics; http://www.cawp.rutgers. edu/

5 Halloran, Liz; "For Republican Women, 2010 is already a huge year"; NPR; June 2, 2010; http://www.npr.org/templates/story/story. php?storyId=127369770

6 Memo written by Rep. Cathy McMorris Rogers to interested parties; Nov. 18, 2010

7 Interview with Debbie Walsh; March 2012

8 Center for Women's Business Research; http://www.womensbusinessresearch.org/

9 Williams, Alex; "The New Math on Campus"; New York Times; Feb. 5, 2010; http://www.nytimes.com/2010/02/07/ fashion/07campus.html?pagewanted=all

10 Emerson, Ramona; "Women use social media more than men: Study"; The Huffington Post; Nov. 23, 2011; http://www.huffingtonpost.com/2011/09/23/women-use-social-media-more_n_978498.html

11 Gobe, Marc; "Emotional Branding, Revised Edition: The New Paradigm for Connecting Brands to People"; Allworth Press; Kindle Edition; April 22, 2010; locations 1540-1545

12 Center for American Women and Politics; http://www.cawp.rutgers. edu/

13 Interview with Rep. Cathy McMorris Rogers; March 21, 2012

14 Divall, Linda and Gutermuth, Randall; American Viewpoint powerpoint; RNC Target Women Project; posted online in 2011-12 but no longer available

15 Interview with Rep. Cathy McMorris Rogers; March 21, 2012

16 Interview with Suzanne Terrell; March 19, 2012

17 Ibid

18 Yarrow, Allison; "She-PAC Targets Democratic Misogynist Hypocrisy, Pushes GOP Women Candidates"; NPR; March 20, 2012

19 Interview with Debbie Walsh; March 2012

20 Interview with Suzanne Terrell; March 19, 2012

21 Ibid

CHAPTER TWELVE

1   eHarmony website; http://www.eharmony.com/about/eharmony/

2   Lopez, Kathryn; "The Love Doctor"; National Review Online; Feb. 14, 2005; http://www.nationalreview.com/articles/213658/love-doctor/interview

3   Shambora, Jessica; "eHarmony's algorithm of love"; CNNMoney; Sept. 23, 2010; http://tech.fortune.cnn.com/2010/09/23/the-algorithm-of-love/

4   eHarmony website

5   Shambora; Sept. 23, 2010

6   Wheeler, William; "The Information Arms Race"; Good; Issue 024; Fall 2011; http://www.good.is/post/the-information-arms-race/

7   Svoboda, Elizabeth; "All Politics is Microtargeting"; Fast Company; Oct. 1, 2008; http://www.fastcompany.com/magazine/129/all-politics-is-micro.html

8   Vega, Tanzina; "Online data helping campaigns customize ads"; New York Times; Feb. 20, 2012; http://www.nytimes.com/2012/02/21/us/politics/campaigns-use-microtargeting-to-attract-supporters.html?pagewanted=all

9   Interview with Terry Benham; March 2012

10   Interview with Clint Reed; April 12, 2012

11   Ibid

12   Svoboda; Oct. 1, 2008

13   Wasserman, David; "Whole Foods vs. Cracker Barrel"; originally published in the Washington Post; published in Arkansas Democrat-Gazette; Dec. 18, 2011

14   Interview with Terry Benham; March 2012

15   Vega; Feb. 20, 2012

CHAPTER FOURTEEN

1   Coy, Peter, Conlin, Michelle, and Herbst, Moira; "The Disposable Worker'"; Business Week; Jan. 7, 2010; http://www.businessweek.com/magazine/content/10_03/b4163032935448.htm

2   Schawbel, Dan; "Me 2.0, Revised and Updated Edition: 4 Steps to Building Your Future"; Kaplan; Kindle Edition; Feb. 20, 2011; locations 533-536

3   Schawbel; locations 1262-1268

4   Beckwith, Harry, and Beckwith, Christine Clifford; "You, Inc."; Warner Business Books; New York; 2007; pages 135-137

5   Interview with Dan Schawbel; April 3, 2012

6   Allen, Nikolas; "How to Become an Opportunity Magnet"; Personal Branding Magazine; August 2011

7   Interview with Dan Schawbel; April 3, 2012

8   Ibid

9   Martin, Tom; "You Are What Google Says You Are"; Personal Branding magazine; February 2011

10 Connolly, Bill; "Brand Your Passion: An Interview with Peter Shankman"; Personal Branding Magazine; August 2011

11 Schawbel; locations 1089-1090

12 Schawbel; locations 317-319

13 Heath, Chip and Heath, Dan; "Made to Stick"; Random House; 2007; pages 19-20, 36-37

14 Schawbel, Dan; "From Nobody to Somebody: An Interview with Tay Zonday"; Personal Branding Magazine; February 2011

15 Taylor, Ivana; "6 Personal Brand Levers to Move Your Audience to Action"; Personal Branding Magazine; August 2011

16 Lindstrom, Martin; "Buyology"; Doubleday; New York; 2008

www.ingramcontent.com/pod-product-compliance
Lightning Source LLC
Chambersburg PA
CBHW051409280526
45785CB00003B/1002